Steaming up to

How the Birmingham to Sutton Coldfield Railway Line was built in 1862

written by Roger Lea

Based on the work of the Sutton Coldfield History Research Group

Contents

Westwood Press Publications

PRINT SHOP, 44 BOLDMERE ROAD, SUTTON COLDFIELD, WEST MIDLANDS B73 5TD

TELEPHONE 021-354 5913

Illustrations

This book is dedicated to Harold Fryer.

ISBN 0 9502636 8 0

 Copyright   First Edition May 1984

Printed and Published by The Westwood Press, Print Shop, 44 Boldmere Road, Sutton Coldfield
West Midlands B73 5TD   Printed by offset litho.

Foreword

Every day thousands travel on the railway line between Sutton and Birmingham, without giving much thought to its origins and history. From Duddeston to Aston their journey is on the route of the first trunk railway in the world, the Grand Junction, but this booklet is concerned with the humbler origins of the five miles from Aston to Sutton. What happened in the twenty-five years between the opening of the Grand Junction in 1837 and the Sutton Branch in 1862? Why choose this particular route rather than others proposed? What were the hopes and fears of its promoters and opponents?

As much a local history as a railway history, I hope it will give general as well as specialist satis-faction. If this booklet is well received, the group will be encouraged to follow up the development of the other Sutton railways, and to consider their history and their effect on Sutton's history, in future publications.

In this account, a number of statements which appear in other histories are contradicted, corrected, or ignored; it is for this reason that the reader is constantly referred to the sources used, so that you can check for yourself. However, neither the research group nor the author is all-knowing, and they will be most interested to receive additional information, comments, and criticisms of any kind.

Roger Lea

Sutton Coldfield from the railroad c. 1863 — Miss Bracken

ACKNOWLEDGMENTS

The Sutton Coldfield History Research Group meets under the auspices of the Workers Educational Association and the Extra-Mural Department of Birmingham University, with the support of Birmingham Public Libraries. As well as the members of the group, many other people have been helpful in supplying information and comments, including Mr G. Hughes of British Rail, Mr E. Talbot, and staff at Sutton Coldfield Library, Birmingham Reference Library, and the Public Record Office, Kew.

I am grateful to Mr G. E. Hughes, 15 Shannon Road, Stafford, for photos of Sutton Station from his collection; to Mr Norman Evans, 23 Walsall Road, Sutton Coldfield, for drawing maps; to Mr J. Horsfall for permission to reproduce the photograph of Penns Hall from his book *The Iron-masters of Penns*; and to the City Librarian of Birmingham for the use of illustrations from the collection at the Local Studies Department of the Central Library, and at Sutton Coldfield Library. Other illustrations are from the author's collection, including the gradient diagram and station plan specially drawn by Stephen Lea. Front cover design and artwork is by Vic Cox, and Douglas Jones wrote the postscript *From Rural Sleepiness to Bustling Activity*.

Cover to the 1858 Western Line plans

THE QUEEN'S HOTEL, NEW STREET STATION, BIRMINGHAM,
LONDON & NORTH WESTERN RAILWAY

CHAPTER ONE

Politics and Personalities

At the beginning of the nineteenth century, canals and turnpike roads were the modern forms of transport, but change was on the way. The Liverpool and Manchester Railway opened in 1830, and in 1833 an Act of Parliament was passed allowing for the building of a railway from Birmingham to Warrington, where it would make a junction with the Liverpool and Manchester Railway at Newton, to be called the Grand Junction Railway. The line was completed in July 1837, and ran via Walsall and Aston to its terminus at Vauxhall.[1] This 78 mile railway was the first trunk line in the world, surveyed by George Stephenson and J. U. Rastrick, and engineered mainly by Joseph Locke. It was built in conjunction with another great trunk line, of which Robert Stephenson was the engineer; work began on the London and Birmingham Railway in 1834, and the first train ran on 17th September 1838 from Euston Station, London, to the

The GJR terminated at Vauxhall (now Duddeston) until its Curzon Street Station was ready. Shelter was provided for the trains, but not for the people! In the background is Duddeston Mill Road bridge.

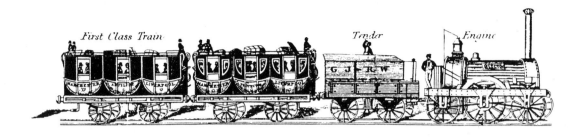

A Grand Junction train of 1838, with outside passengers and luggage in the stage-coach style.

terminus in Birmingham at Curzon Street. These lines merged in 1846 to form the London and North Western Railway Company (LNWR).

R. K. Dent's *Old and New Birmingham* (1880) gives the following account of Birmingham's first train:[2]

"Early on Tuesday morning, July 4th 1837, the town (of Birmingham) was in a state of commotion... At seven o'clock precisely the bell rang when the leading train drawn by the 'Wildfire' engine commenced moving. The train consisted of eight carriages, all first class, and bearing the following names, 'Triumph', 'Greyhound', 'Swallow', 'Liverpool and Birmingham Mail', 'Celerity', 'Umpire', 'Statesman', and 'Birmingham and Manchester Mail'. It started slowly, but emerging from the yard at Vauxhall speedily burst off at a rapid rate. To those who for the first time witnessed such a scene it was peculiarly exciting, and the immense multitude, as far as the eye could reach, gave expression to their admiration by loud and long-continued huzzas, and the waving of hats and handkerchiefs."

People were not long in becoming accustomed to the new mode and speed of travelling, and consequently when the London and Birmingham line opened the following year there was considerably less excitement. In 1839 the Birmingham and Derby Junction Railway was opened, connecting Derby to the London and Birmingham at Hampton-in-Arden, and three years later the line from the

company's Birmingham terminus at Lawley Street via Saltley and Castle Bromwich, meeting their existing line at Whitacre, was opened. This line, known as the Tame Valley Line, became part of the Midland Railway Company (MR) on its formation in 1844.

The map in Figure (i) shows how the area was served with railways in 1842, and Suttonians soon began to be concerned about the relative isolation of the town.[3] Although there were canal wharves at Minworth and Gravelly Hill, and stations at Castle Bromwich and Perry Barr, coal was carted from the pitheads at Brownhills[4] and the extra costs of transporting lime, stone, bricks and timber over the bumpy, muddy roads put Sutton tradesmen at a disadvantage. The transport of fragile manufactured goods by cart was hazardous, and Mr Holbeche, who "had lived within the parish for more than half a century...remembered when the roads to Birmingham were impassable, when the roads to Walsall were impassable, and when to get to Coleshill they had to go a round of many miles."[5]

The advantages of laying a railway line from Sutton to join either the LNWR or the MR were clear—coal could be carried to Sutton from either the South Staffordshire or Derby coalfields, there-

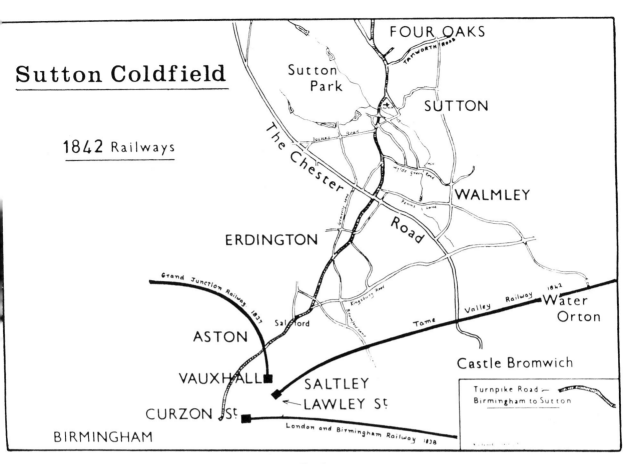

Fig. (i)

by reducing its price, and pleasure traffic from Birmingham and other places to Sutton Park would be increased.[6]

At the time of the opening of the Grand Junction Railway in 1837, that company had plans for a Derby branch which would have served Sutton, following the route of the Ebrook valley and then the present Lichfield line, but this was not pursued.[7]

Then on 16th September 1845, at a meeting at the Hen and Chickens Hotel in Birmingham, the Birmingham and Lichfield Railway Company was formed.[8] This company lasted two days, as on the 18th the Board met the projectors of the Lichfield and Manchester Railway in Lichfield, and amalgamated with them to form the Birmingham, Lichfield and Manchester Railway Company (BL&MR), with the MP for North Warwickshire, Richard Spooner, as Chairman. This was at the height of the 'Railway Mania'. The BL&MR appointed John R. McLean as their surveyor, and he reported in

October 1845 on two possible routes between Birmingham and Lichfield; one, which was adopted, would have left the Grand Junction a few hundred yards west of Aston station, would have crossed the eastern end of the cemetery, proceeding west of Witton Lakes following the valley across College Road and Kings Road, entering Sutton Park just north of Banners Gate, and so west of Little Aston and Shenstone to join the Trent Valley Line at Lichfield.[9] The other route was through Erdington and Sutton. McLean said, "I should recommend the Sutton Coldfield line if that town were a place of much importance, but as I understand it has little trade, and principally composed of an agricultural population, to whom rapid conveyance is not essential, I would advise you to adopt the line through Sutton Park." News of this decision caused uproar in Sutton, and a town meeting was held at the Moot Hall on 14th September. This meeting passed a long resolution beginning,

7

"This meeting has heard with surprise and regret, that after all the notices which appeared relative to the Birmingham, Lichfield and Manchester Railway Company promising in distinct terms the necessary advantages to the town of Sutton Coldfield, this line is now projected to run at a distance which will entirely preclude the inhabitants from any advantages arising from railway communication..."

In order to prevent opposition to their Bill, the BL&MR promised to build a branch from their line to Sutton, and the Act of Parliament was duly passed in July 1846.[10]

On 15th August 1846 the newly-formed LNWR offered to buy the shares of the BL&MR for £2 each, and in September the BL&MR was taken over.[11] The LNWR engineer, Joseph Locke, surveyed a route to the east of Erdington and Sutton in response to representations from 'persons of the Parish of Sutton Coldfield', and an Act of Parliament for this amended line was obtained in 1847. These lines are shown in Figure (ii).

Sutton was governed under the terms of its 1528 Charter by a Warden and Society, roughly equivalent to a Mayor and Corporation, and it was the 1845 Warden, Joseph Pimlot Oates, who had presented the resolution to the BL&MR Board. The eventual agreement reached between the BL&MR and the Warden and Society, on 22nd April 1846, was in the form of a bond, which the LNWR also agreed to observe, to build the railway within five years avoiding Sutton Park, with a first class station at Sutton, or pay a penalty of £20,000.[12] Almost immediately after the 1847 Act "there was a great change in the financial state of affairs in England and a very large number of the lines granted in 1846 and 1847 were never made at all."[13] Years went by and no start was made on the line, the five-year period was extended to seven years until eventually in 1853 there were negotiations to liquidate the bond. There was some quibbling as to whether the bond referred principally to the avoiding of the Park (in which case no penalty was due) or the building of the line (in which case £20,000 was to be paid)[14] and whether the Warden

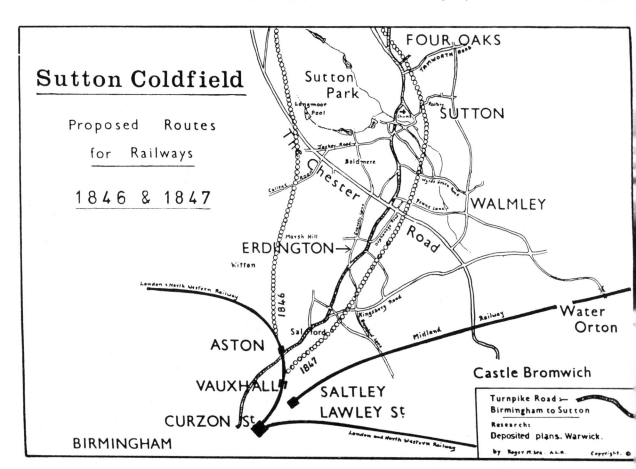

Fig. (ii) — Both lines would have crossed open country—neither Nechells nor Aston were yet built up.

and Society would still be entitled to bring an action against the LNWR for failure to build the line even though the bond were liquidated. A figure of £3,000 was agreed on, and the Warden and Society used the money to build a new town hall; the architect was G. Bidlake of Wolverhampton, whose more famous son, W. H. Bidlake, was a noted member of the arts and crafts movement and designed several Sutton houses. The Town Hall was opened on 27th September 1859, and still stands in Mill Street, now known as the Masonic Buildings.[15]

As soon as the LNWR abandoned their plans in 1853, with the lapse of their powers under the Act of Parliament, other schemes were proposed. One idea was put forward by Alderman Samuel Beale in July 1853. He was an Ironmaster, former Mayor of Birmingham, deputy Chairman of the MR (later Chairman) soon to be elected MP for Derby.[16] He and other public-spirited men of Birmingham were very concerned to provide proper facilities for the recreation of the working classes, and the proposal was put to the Warden and Society by the Mayor of Birmingham, James Baldwin; it was to build a crystal palace in Sutton Park and connect it by railway to the Midland line at Saltley.[17] The plan was opposed because the terms for using the Park were unsatisfactory, and a petition against it signed by over 400 Suttonians was raised after unauthorised press statements by one of the members of the Society. The proposal was not pursued, and some years later Aston Hall and Park were purchased by a Birmingham Company as "a place of recreation for the inhabitants of the Borough."[18]

These events coloured later developments in several ways, not only on the question of the route to be taken by a railway, but also as regards attitudes. A petition against the 1847 Act included the sentence, "Any railway would make it (Sutton) a smoky and degraded suburb of Birmingham,"[19] and this antipathy to railways is expressed by Miss Bracken in her 1860 *History of the Forest and Chase of Sutton Coldfield:*

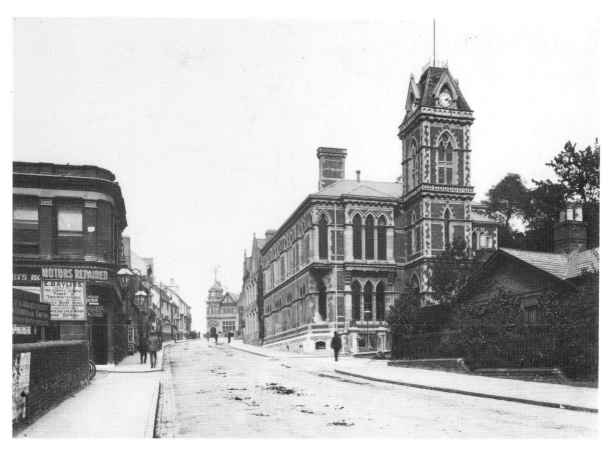

The 1859 Town Hall—the clock tower was taken down in 1970.

"Long may it (the Sutton Coldfield air) be worth the seeking—long may the gallant old Beacon hold his ramparts against the sappers and miners of the West, and the Tame stretch out lines of defence against dark cohorts from the South! Sutton may readily be spoiled... At the present time there is not a steam engine in the parish."[20]

Some of the Sutton gentry, Messrs Mendham, Steele Perkins, and Sadler, who owned property along the present Lichfield line, wrote to the LNWR to try to get the route diverted away from their land.[21] At the 1859 Inquiry both sides were at pains to prove that there was then no opposition to the principle of the railway connection, and the two gentlemen who became the leading protagonists in the attempt to get a railway line to Sutton both felt there were lessons to be learned.

One was William Kirkpatrick Riland Bedford (1826—1905), who became Rector of Sutton in 1850, and was Warden in 1854 and 1855. He was also a prominent freemason, and he founded the Free Foresters Cricket Club. He lived in style at the Rectory in Rectory Park, and both as Rector and privately he owned considerable property in Sutton. Although he was often unwell from 1856 onwards, he took an active interest in local affairs and local history, and his standard history of the town was published in 1890; he caused the transcript to be made of the Railway Bill Enquiry which is now in Sutton Coldfield Library. At the

Rev. W. K. R. Bedford

September 1858 meeting, he said, "there were some gentlemen, whose names did not appear in the prospectuses, who did all they could to keep a railway away, and to get as little as possible out of this colossal Company for their breach of faith."[22]

The Rectory stood in Rectory Park.

Penns in 1860, facing South

At the same September meeting the fear was expressed that the LNWR would be equally faithless again, and this attitude was shared by the other leading light in these events, Mr Baron Dickenson Webster, (1818—1860). He lived at Penns Hall, and had a large wire-making business at Penns Mill and Plants Forge, to which a railway connection would be very useful. However, his interest seems to have been wider and philanthropic as well,

"This lavish and open-handed liberality to all and sundry was combined with a flair for civic administration and the energy to take on any function the local citizens saw fit to ask of him. He combined all this with a tact and gentle charm which won all hearts, and he was known and venerated by the entire district from the humblest to the highest."[23]

He had represented the Warden and Society in the negotiations over the liquidation of the £20,000 bond, the LNWR being represented by Samuel Carter. Webster later described the meeting, "Mr Carter said what do you want, we will give you a £10 note for your bond. Mr Carter said that to me."[24] His distaste for the big companies was compounded by the interview with the LNWR Board in 1857 (see below). Baron Webster met three Birmingham business men in October 1853 to discuss forming an independent company, but the impending Crimean War made the investment impossible.[25] So ended talk of a line to Sutton for a few years.

Meanwhile, during the year 1849 a large area in the older part of Birmingham was cleared for the erection of a central railway station to replace the three earlier terminus stations of Vauxhall, Curzon Street and Lawley Street. It involved the demolition of many worn-out and tumble-down buildings in Peck Lane, The Froggary, Little Colmore Street and King Street; it took five years to build and was opened on 1st June 1854, named New Street Station.[26] This made the prospect of a rail link to Sutton even more attractive to potential promoters, and meant that the agreement of the MR and the LNWR would be necessary for running into the new central station, since it was subject to various covenants, though owned by the LNWR.[27]

The frontage of the new station was taken up by the Queens Hotel, and it was here in June 1857 that the question of a rail link to Sutton was re-opened. The meeting had been called by a public notice issued by several prominent citizens, including Baron Webster, who took the chair, to ascertain what support there would be for such a railway. The meeting empowered Webster, who was Warden that year, and Thomas Aurelius Attwood, of Wood End House, Erdington (son of Thomas Attwood the banker, first MP for Birmingham and campaigner for reform) to negotiate with the two big companies.[28] A few days later they attended, by appointment, a meeting of the LNWR

Board in London, and Baron Webster later described the encounter:

"We were introduced and there was a very full Board of Directors present, Lord Chandos in the Chair. The first question which was asked was, I believe, 'Have you made any communication with the Midland Railway on this subject?' Our answer was, no! Then after conferring among themselves for a few moments they said, 'Before we give you an answer we must understand what our good friends the Midland Company have to say about it—having done so we will communicate with you again...' then we took up our hats, bowed, and went away."[29]

On 18th August 1857 the LNWR wrote to Baron Webster saying that the directors were not prepared to find the necessary capital, but if an independent company was set up the new line could be connected to its system and the LNWR would operate it provided it was constructed to the approval of the Company Engineer and that it did not make a loss. In a further letter they agreed to two of their directors, Admiral Moorsom and Mr Ledsam, being directors of the proposed independent company, but still offered no better terms.[30] These facts were reported to a meeting at New Street on 26th September 1857 by Attwood, and were considered discouraging since all the funds would have to be raised locally and in any case it was too late to obtain an Act in that session of Parliament. A provisional committee was set up, consisting of B. D. Webster, Admiral Moorsom, Joseph Ledsam, T. A. Attwood, Richard Spooner (MP for North Warwickshire), Josiah Mason of Erdington, W. K. Riland Bedford, Thomas Chavasse of Wylde Green, William Fowler of Erdington, J. Y. Robins of Allesley Park, R. Fowler, V. Holbeche, and C. Couchman.[31] This committee did little, leaving the business in the hands of its Chairman, Baron Webster, and the Secretary, Alderman T. R. T. Hodgson.

Early the following year, 1858, possible routes for a line were being surveyed by Henry Columbus Hurry for the provisional board,[32] but also by promoters who had the support of the Midland Railway for a line from Bromford Lane to Sutton. Two of these men, Burke and Manning, were friends of William Fowler, senior, of Birches Green, Erdington. He was a surveyor as his father and

New Street Station in 1854

grandfather had been, and his son was surveyor to the Eastern line (see below); many of the parish tithe maps of the district bear his name. He was a railway enthusiast, keen to get a line built since the heady days of 1846, and many of his friends were involved in various of the lines being made in the Midlands. He arranged for Baron Webster to meet the surveyor of the newly projected line, James Baird Burke, in the summer of 1858.

Webster quickly organised his associates to form a company with this line in mind, which would connect his mills with the outside world. He wrote to Alderman Hodgson, explaining that a line east of the turnpike road was the only one he could support, and asking him to convene a meeting of all those who had been interested the previous year, so that he could extricate himself from the provisional committee with its LNWR

links.[33] He took the Chair at this meeting, 26th August 1858, at the Union Hotel, Union Street, and explained his position. Apart from the line he favoured and recommended, the meeting considered two lines from the LNWR at Aston, one east and one west of the main road; all three lines would be single track. The resolution eventually passed was,

''That with the view of determining the relative merits of the three several lines of railway proposed and starting either from the LNWR or the MR, this meeting be adjourned until 23rd of September next, and in the meantime the LNWR be requested to state what support they will give to either of the two lines proposed in connection with their railway.''[34]

Baron Webster and his friends, however, having declared their position, walked down to Mr Fowler's office in Waterloo Street and immediately issued the following prospectus:[35]

Birmingham, Erdington, & Sutton-Coldfield Railway.

CAPITAL £60,000,

IN 6,000 SHARES OF £10 EACH.—DEPOSIT £1 PER SHARE.

The Liability of the Shareholders will be limited by the Act to the amount of their Shares

Provisional Directors.

Chairman—SIR JOHN RATCLIFF, Mayor of Birmingham.

Deputy Chairman—BARON D. WEBSTER, ESQ., Penns Sutton-Coldfield.

JOSIAH MASON, ESQ. Erdington, Birmingham.	WILLIAM FOWLER, ESQ., Birches Green, Birmingham.
THOS. S. CHEVASSE, ESQ., Wylde Green, Sutton-Coldfield.	ZACCHEUS WALKER, ESQ., Birmingham.
ABRAHAM DIXON. ESQ., Birches Green, Birmingham.	GEORGE BODDINGTON, ESQ., Driffield House, Sutton-Coldfield.
G. R. ELKINGTON. ESQ., Birmingham.	ABEL ROLLASON, ESQ., Shepherd's Green House, Erdington.
CHARLES SHAW, ESQ., Edgbaston, Birmingham.	

With power to add to their number.

Bankers.

THE BIRMINGHAM AND MIDLAND BANKING COMPANY, Birmingham.

Engineer.

JAMES B. BURKE, ESQ.

Solicitor	Local Solicitors.
W. T. MANNING, ESQ., 20, Great George Street. Westminster.	Messrs. HOLBECHE & ADDENBROOKE, Sutton-Coldfield.

Secretary.

MR. EDWARD CARTER.

THE district of country lying between Birmingham and Sutton-Coldfield now stands in urgent need of Railway accommodation; it having, in fact, become a suburb of Birmingham, which is daily extending itself in this locality.

With the view of supplying the deficiency, the landowners of the district and residents of Birmingham, with the sanction and support of the Midland Railway Company, have formed themselves into a Company for the purpose of promoting this Railway.

To accomplish this object, the construction of less than five miles of new Railway is required by forming a Junction with the Midland Railway, near Erdington Hall, keeping on the Eastern side of the Turnpike Road, passing by Gravelly Hill, through Erdington, and thence by Wylde Green to Sutton Coldfield.

The course of the line has been carefully examined, and can be traversed by moderate gradients without any works of magnitude. It has been selected after mature consideration as to the requirements of the district and the cost of construction, and the Provisional Directors are satisfied, from the Report of the Engineer, that the line adopted is in all respects the best calculated to carry out these objects.

Every year more fully proves that the inhabitants of large manufacturing towns are availing themselves of the facilities afforded by Railways to reside away from but still within easy reach of business, and few of the principal cities in England demand such Railway accommodation so much as Birmingham.

The district of country from Gravelly Hill and Erdington to Sutton possesses advantages beyond any other in the neighbourhood of Birmingham, and so much has this been felt, that, although without Railway accommodation, buildings of the first class have rapidly sprung into existence, and the whole country for some distance on each side of the proposed line is now being sold as building land. In such a locality it is all important to have constant Railway communication for passengers to the centre of Birmingham, and fortunately this will be fully provided for by the proposed Junction with the Midland Railway running into New Street Station, thus giving to this short branch the benefit of the great outlay incurred in the formation of the latter Terminus, whilst by being placed upon the Railway system the facilities for agricultural purposes and for procuring cheap coal will be secured.

The far famed Park at Sutton Coldfield, containing upwards of 2,000 acres, possesses natural attractions so far beyond any other in the vicinity of Birmingham, that it has always been a favorite resort; and it is a very important feature of this project, that it will afford hourly communication to the Park, at an expense within the reach of all classes.

The Station at Sutton will be within a few minutes' walk of the Park, and it is proposed so to arrange with the Corporation of Sutton, that the ticket available for the Railway shall also admit into the Park, by which means all delay or trouble will be avoided.

An arrangement for working the line has been submitted to the Midland Railway Company, under which a clear fifty per cent. of the gross receipts of this line will be handed over to the Shareholders, and that Company have stated that they should be willing to adopt such an agreement. Under so favorable an arrangement, having regard to the existing traffic, which has been carefully estimated, and the various sources of increase, there can be no doubt that the proposed line will be of a most remunerative character.

Applications for Shares, in the following form, may be addressed to the Secretary, at the offices of the Company, 23, Waterloo Street, Birmingham:—

To the Provisional Directors of The Birmingham, Erdington, and Sutton-Coldfield Railway.

Gentlemen,

I request that you will allot me   Shares in the above Railway, and I hereby undertake to accept the same, or any less number which you may allot, and to pay the deposit thereon, and to sign the Subscribers' Agreement when required.

Dated the   day of   1858.

On 26th August, Attwood had been in Paris and the Rector at the seaside,[36] but when they returned those who favoured a line from the LNWR west of the turnpike road rallied to them. A deputation from the Eastern Company attended a meeting of the Warden and Society of Sutton on 13th September to enlist their support, but by then a rival Western Company was forming, and a decision was deferred until they had received a deputation from the other line.[37] By the time of the public meeting of the 23rd September, support for the rival lines had polarised, and the meeting, at which Riland Bedford presided, was not attended by many of the supporters of the Eastern Line. Riland Bedford was able to inform the meeting that the LNWR was giving more support and encouragement than it had the previous year, being prepared to operate the line at cost, with 50% of the takings going to the independent company.[38] Shortly afterwards the following prospectus was issued:

Birmingham, Erdington, & Sutton Coldfield Railway Company,

WESTERN LINE.

CAPITAL, £60,000,

In 6,000 Shares of £10 each. — Deposit £1 per Share; and no further Call to be made, unless the Act be obtained.

The Liability of the Shareholders will **be limited by the Act** to the amount of their **Shares.**

Provisional Directors.

THOMAS AURELIUS ATTWOOD, Esq., Wood End House, Erdington.
The REV. W. K. RILAND BEDFORD, Rector of Sutton Coldfield.
WILLIAM LUCY, Esq., Edgbaston.
ADMIRAL MOORSOM, Highfield, Edgbaston,
JOSEPH FREDERICK LEDSAM, Esq., Chad Hill, Edgbaston, } *Directors of the London*
MATTHEW LYON, Esq., Forebridge, Stafford, } *and*
} *North Western Railway Company.*
HENRY ELWELL, Esq., Church Hill House, Handsworth.
JOSIAH YEOMANS ROBINS, Esq., Allesley Park.
JAMES HUGHES, Esq., Sutton Coldfield.
EDWIN GWYTHER, Esq., Edgbaston.
JOHN WIGGAN, Esq., Sutton Coldfield.
JOHN BUGGINS, Esq., Sutton Coldfield.
JOHN BREARLEY PAYN, Esq., Grove House, Handsworth.
With power to add to their number.

Bankers.

MESSRS. ATTWOODS, SPOONER, & CO., Birmingham.
MESSRS. SPOONER, ATTWOODS, & CO., London.

Solicitors.   ### Engineer.
MESSRS. HODGSON & ALLEN.   H. C. HURRY, ESQ.
MR. HENRY LUDLOW.

Surveyor.   ### Secretary.
MR. JOSEPH LUDLOW.   MR. W. LOMAS HARRISON.

The populous district between Birmingham, Erdington, and Sutton Coldfield being without means of transit, either for passengers or goods, other than the Turnpike Road from Birmingham, has long felt the want of Railway accommodation. With a view to supply this requirement several meetings of the owners of property and residents have been held within the last two years, and a Committee was formed for the purpose of arranging the best mode of carrying out their views, but in consequence of the depressed state of the money market it has been from time to time deemed advisable to postpone active operations.

Engineers and Surveyors were, however, instructed to ascertain the best Line; Surveys were made, and levels taken on both sides of the Turnpike Road, and it is found that a Line of Railway commencing at the Aston Station, of the London and North Western Railway, thence running nearly parallel with the Turnpike Road on its western side, to terminate within a short distance of Sutton Park and the centre of the Town of Sutton, is the best, being the cheapest and the shortest route from Birmingham to Sutton, and affords on its way the greatest amount of accommodation to one of the most populous and increasing suburbs of Birmingham, and certainly the most eligible for building purposes.

Such is the Line this Company now proposes to construct: it will not exceed five miles in length, and is most favorable as regards curves and gradients.

It is obvious that any Railway, to really benefit the population, should be in connection and alliance with the London and North Western Railway Company, in order to secure the important privilege of using the New Street Station, at Birmingham, and a direct communication with the populous and mineral district of South Staffordshire, which will afford a good and cheap supply of Coal, Lime, &c., to the District through which the Line passes.

Convenient Stations at Gravelly Hill, Erdington, Chester Road, Maney, and Sutton, will be provided near to the Turnpike Road.

The London and North Western Railway Company have consented to co-operate in obtaining the Act of Parliament, and they will arrange to work the Line when made, at the cost of the mere working expenses, which they undertake shall not exceed 50 per cent. of the gross receipts.

A careful investigation of the Traffic has been made, and it is evident that with the favourable terms obtained from the London and North Western Railway Company, should only a moderate proportion be transferred to the intended Railway, it would secure an ample return upon the Capital to be expended.

===

Applications for Shares may be addressed in the following form to the Secretary, at the Offices of the London and North Western Railway Company, New Street, Birmingham :—

FORM OF APPLICATION.

To the Provisional Committee of The Birmingham, Erdington, and Sutton Coldfield Railway Company, (Western Line.)

I request that you will allot me   *Shares of £10 each in the above Railway, and I undertake to accept the same, or any less number which may be allotted me, and to pay the deposit thereon, and to sign the Subscription Contract when required.*

Dated the   *day of*   1858.

Name in full ....

Address ....

Occupation ....

Resolved. That the Assent of this Corporation be given to the proposed Railway called the Birmingham Erdington and Sutton Coldfield (Western Line) this Meeting feeling satisfied that the proposed (Western line) will afford every accommodation as a passenger and traffic line, which the Inhabitants of this Parish can require.

Warden & Society minutes, 27th September 1858

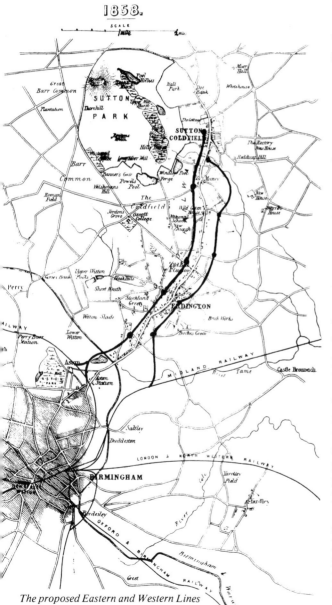

1858.

The proposed Eastern and Western Lines

On 27th September a deputation from the Western Line was received by the Warden and Society, and after long discussion it was,

> "Resolved. That the Assent of this Corporation be given to the proposed Railway called the Birmingham Erdington and Sutton Coldfield (Western Line). This Meeting feeling satisfied that the proposed (Western Line) will afford every accommodation as a passenger and traffic line which the Inhabitants of this Parish can require."

This was carried by 11 votes to 6; Baron Webster, as Warden, did not vote, although many of the 17 who did were also interested parties, standing to gain either as shareholders or by the increased value of their property, from one line or the other.

Both companies proceeded to solicit support, and both produced Bills for the 1858—9 Parliamentary session. However, the division caused men who would far rather have been allies in promoting a line to be rivals,[39] and attempts were made to combine the two companies. In October two directors from each side met at Mr Attwood's bank—Attwood, Shaw, Webster and Payn—and agreed to a suggestion of the Rector's that an independent surveyor decide which route would be best.[40] This was defeated at the next meeting of the Western Board apparently because there was no written proof of the Eastern Board's agreement, but since Admiral Moorsom, the LNWR director, advised this course of action, the LNWR may already have been committed to their line.[41]

Constantine Richard Moorsom (1792—1861), son of an admiral, made rapid progress in the Navy through his ingenuity in improving guns and modifying ships. He had been on the Board of the London and Birmingham Railway, of which his brother William was a surveyor, and became an active member of the Board of the LNWR, taking charge of several of the subsidiary lines. He was made deputy Chairman in April 1858, and, when Lord Chandos retired in 1861, was Chairman for a few weeks until his sudden death; he is supposed to be responsible for the naval style of railwaymen's uniforms.[42] Although he remains a shadowy figure in Sutton railway affairs, his rôle was possibly crucial: if the initiative of the Eastern Company in issuing a prospectus arose from a desire to force the pace, and impatience with the desultory progress of the provisional committee, with the ebullient Baron Webster at the helm; and if the Western represented the more cautious spirits who wished to stay with the big company, with the conservative Riland Bedford as their Chairman; then the LNWR stood for its own commercial interest, which was to wait and see which side would win and then absorb it at leisure, with Admiral Moorsom in the rôle of Svengali. But for him, the two sides may well have resolved their differences: as Riland Bedford observed, each side was strong enough to cut the other's throat, but too weak to succeed without help.[43]

In January 1859 the Western Line initiated a discussion at Dee's Hotel, but the only suggestion made was that both Bills should be withdrawn and a mutually acceptable line agreed in time for the 1860 session of Parliament—the Eastern Company however felt that they had gone too far to withdraw now. The position was discussed at a meeting of the LNWR Board on 11th June 1859, when it was reported that proposals made to the Eastern Company had not been accepted—no details of this proposal survive. Thereupon the Board instructed their Engineer, Joseph Errington (who had, incidentally, been employed by the defunct BL&MR) to adopt the Western Line Bill as their own, and take over the company.[44]

A select committee of the House of Commons was appointed to approve one or other of the Bills for further reading, and this met from 4th—7th July 1859. The proceedings of this committee, where all the main protagonists—Webster,

FRONT OF THE NEW GRAND CENTRAL RAILWAY STATION, AT BIRMINGHAM.

Attwood, Fowler, Riland Bedford, Ludlow, Burke and Hurry—testified, is the source of most of this booklet. Many points were discussed, but in an unreal atmosphere since the LNWR had adopted the Western line at the end of June, too late for the MR to adopt the Eastern, and this was felt on both sides to be decisive. The LNWR would make it double track, and they owned New Street Station, then only half its later size, with only two lines through the tunnel. The junction at the Proofing House (where there was a ticket platform) was safer than the MR junction at Lawley Street, where main line trains would be running at speed;[45]

conclusively, finance would be no problem. The Committee reported accordingly, and on 8th August 1859 the 'London and North Western Railway, Sutton Coldfield Branch Act' received the Royal Assent.

In the autumn of 1859 Penns Mill closed and the business transferred to new premises at Hay Mills, near Small Heath. On 8th August 1860 the contract for making the line was signed by Messrs Eckersley and Read of Newport, and the line opened on 2nd June 1862, fulfilling the clause in the Act requiring the Branch to be built within three years.

ATTWOOD & SPOONERS BANK, NEW ST.

CHAPTER TWO

The Route

ASTON

The Aston Viaduct of the Grand Junction Railway, crossing the Fazeley Canal and the Lichfield Turnpike Road, was one of the beauties of the line. The curve of the railway at this point was necessitated by the reluctance of the owner of Aston Hall, James Watt, son of the great engineer, to allow the line to pass over (or under) his land. There was originally no station at Aston, but with the rapid growth of the population a station was built, destroying the beauty of the viaduct, but serving the visitors flocking to Aston Hall when it was purchased as a pleasure park in 1856.

Joseph Locke's 1847 line would have branched off at Nechells, not at that time built up, which was more convenient for his route east of the turnpike road, but by 1858 Nechells was thickly populated and Aston was the first open country;[1] there was never any question that if the line were to connect to the LNWR, Aston Station was the desirable place. There were advantages in connecting to the LNWR —there was easy access to New Street Station and the London trains, and Suttonians and Erdingtonians preferred Black Country coal to the Derbyshire and Leicestershire coal carried on the MR;[2] it served a populous district of potential day trippers, whereas only a minority of the people had connections in the Derby direction, the MR passing through a predominantly rural area—but in the event one of the main advantages turned out to be the popularity of the line with the vast numbers of people who came to live at Aston.

The Aston Viaduct (Aston Station opened in 1854)

Aston junction

ACROSS THE TAME VALLEY

The line branches off at Aston on a high embankment, originally to cross the Tame by a wooden trestle viaduct, being a single track line, but the LNWR built a more substantial brick viaduct of five arches for their double-track line. Another junction was planned here, for a spur line forming the third side of a triangle, so that traffic from the Perry Barr direction could gain access to the Sutton Branch. The idea was evidently abandoned, possibly because of the expense of another Tame crossing, possibly difficulties were experienced in making the embankment—Joseph Locke had had great trouble with the Grand Junction in the same area twenty years earlier—

possibly it was decided to delay building it until a better estimate of the likely traffic could be made. The embankment was described as "Very heavy works", and would have been avoided by the 1846 BL&MR line which would have branched off near Brookvale Road.[3]

The Canal viaduct. These arches, like those of the Tame viaduct, are on a curve as well as being skew, making for complicated brickwork.

The Tame viaduct, overshadowed by the Aston Expressway.

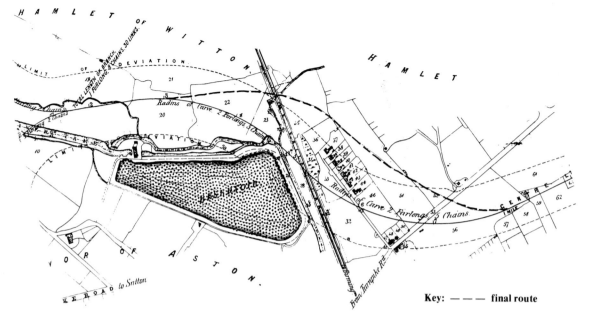

The 1858 Plan (above) shows the line much closer to the reservoir.

Houses in Copeley Hill (photo c. 1928)

In his original survey, Henry Columbus Hurry had planned to take the line round the reservoir in front of the hill, crossing Slade Road near the present traffic island on a bridge of only 25 feet span (it being "only a back road"), and the canal on a 40 foot viaduct. After crossing the canal, the incline would have been 1:88. Strong objections were made to this route by the Birmingham Waterworks Company (this being their main reservoir and pumping station at the time) and by the residents of the big houses in Copeley Terrace (later Copeley Hill, now straddled by Spaghetti Junction).[4] A deviation was made to the present route, with its three-arch viaduct over the canal and the bridge over Slade Road supporting a substantial embankment; the incline is 1:95. The bulk of the Act of Parliament is taken up with provisions to safeguard the canal and the waterworks.

The projected Eastern Line would have branched off the MR opposite Common Lane, proceeding on a high embankment across water meadows

Erdington Hall

(now factories);[5] the embankments and the viaducts were planned to be wide enough for a double-track line, even though only a single track would be laid in the first instance.[6] The viaducts over the Tame and the Fazeley Canal would bring the line into the land of Erdington Hall, which was then a farm rented by Mr Wheelwright from Mr Brace-bridge; only a farm track needed to be bridged,[7] Tyburn Road not then existing. The present Wheelwright Road would be crossed by an over-bridge, and from there to Kingsbury Road the land pertained to Wood End House; here the line,

from being on a 10 foot embankment, plunged into a 30 foot cutting, the gradient for the whole distance from the river being 1:70. At Wood End House lived Mr Attwood, a Director of the Western Company, and he petitioned against the line although it would have passed 300 yards away from the house on the other side of an ornamental lake and a plantation. At Wood End Cottage lived Mr Fowler (not William Fowler) who had ''very ornamental grounds'', but did not object to the line.[8]

Wood End House

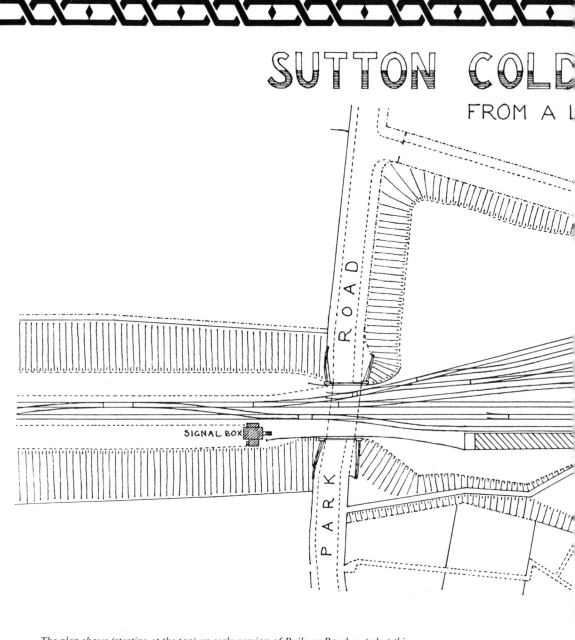

SUTTON COLD

FROM A L

ROAD

SIGNAL BOX

PARK

FEE

The plan shows (starting at the top) an early version of Railway Road, gated at this period, and the embankments, many of which were replaced by brick retaining walls in 1884 (but the gateposts to the Council House grounds in the present Railway Road may be original). The coal offices were erected as required over a period of time, but the goods shed, cattle docks, crane and wagon turntables are probably original. The refreshment rooms and their canopy had been added by 1868, and the signal box was added some time after the refreshment rooms. Station Street was the new name for Hackett Street, and by 1866 there was a Railway Tavern in Station Street and a Railway Inn in High Street, as well as the Station Hotel.

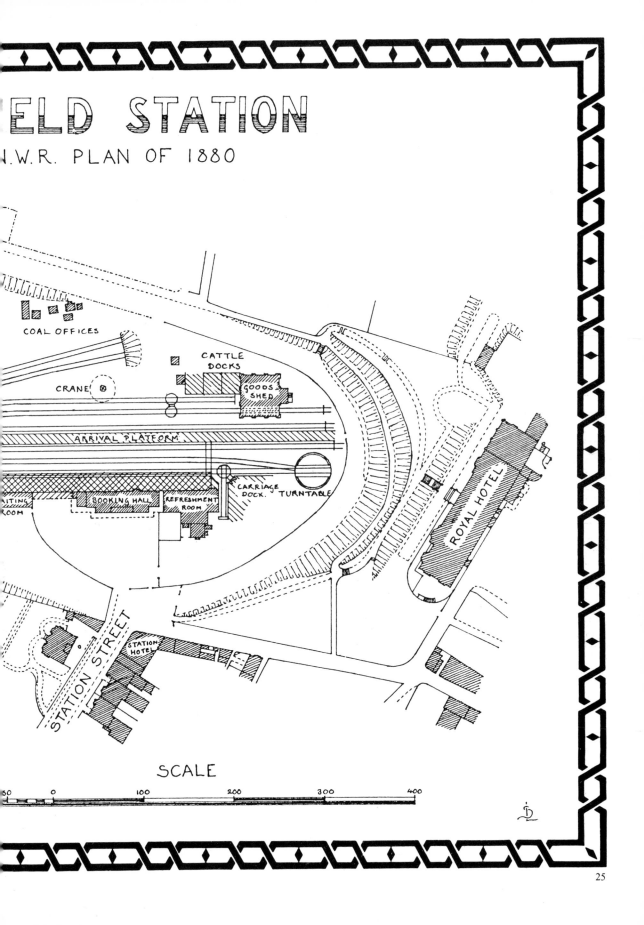

ELD STATION

N.W.R. PLAN OF 1880

COAL OFFICES

CATTLE DOCKS

CRANE ⊗

GOODS SHED

ARRIVAL PLATFORM

CARRIAGE DOCK. TURNTABLE

WAITING ROOM

BOOKING HALL

REFRESHMENT ROOM

ROYAL HOTEL

STATION STREET

STATION HOTEL

SCALE

50   0   100   200   300   400

Looking up the incline through Hillaries Road bridge and Gravelly Hill Station.

Gravelly Hill. Detail of footbridge.

GRAVELLY HILL

The original 1858 plan was for a single-track station on a 1:88 incline, which James Baird Burke, the surveyor of the Eastern Line, objected to as unsafe. Even the existing double track 1:95 station presented starting and stopping problems to the early trains, and the Board of Trade Inspector asked for catch points with a blind siding to be provided below the station on the uphill side. A possible site for this siding can still be seen on the embankment east of Slade Road. In 1859 some building was taking place on both sides of the line; to the east, all the way to Birches Green, there were "beautiful sites for building", "calculated for villa residences", while to the west the land was "more adapted to 1 or 2 acre plots and not so large a class of house"—most of the land was up for sale as building land.[9] An argument for the Western Line was that the villa residents, having their own carriages, would have less need for the railway than the less wealthy tenants of the smaller houses. Hillaries Road did not exist in 1859, and

The Booking Office—the earliest building is the only one to have survived.

Hunton Hill was not developed, but both bridges are original. As to the station, a plan of 1914 shows a number of buildings, but they may not all be original. On the up or Birmingham platform there were five waiting rooms of various kinds, some in the rustic wood panel style of the other stations on the line, but two on the ground floor of the booking office. The booking office is at first floor level, but owing to the depth of the cutting, it appears to be a single storey building from the Frederick Road side; it is level with the footbridge, which may therefore be contemporary in spite of being numbered 6a. There was only one waiting room on the up side, which suggests that most of the passengers were going to and from Birmingham, not requiring waiting room facilities on the way home. Initially the signals were operated outside in the open, but the signal cabin would have been installed about 1870 when the signalling arrangements were modernised. The original height of the platforms was 20 inches

A once immaculate station going back to nature.

L. & N. W. R.
GRAVELLY HILL

Plan of 1914, showing five up-platform waiting rooms.

above track level, compared with the present 30 inches. Only the brick booking-office building remains of the buildings shown on the plan.

The Eastern Line station would have been on a curve of 16 chains radius in a cutting 30 feet deep near the junction of Kingsbury Road and Wood End Lane, the track being on the level. Access to it was intended to be gained by making a road from Gravelly Hill, and this would have crossed the land of Thomas Ryland, an agricultural chemist. He petitioned against the line on the grounds that his privacy would be destroyed because porters and station-men would be his neighbours, and even a public house might be built nearby. He had rebuilt his house to villa standards (it still stands, now a children's home called St Johns) and he

The Redlands, Gravelly Hill.
Home of the late Mr Thomas Ryland,
now St. John's Home.

wanted nothing to change; his arguments were refuted when it was pointed out that all the surrounding land was on sale for building in any case, and there was nothing to stop the owner of the adjacent land from building "pig styes or cottages close to Mr Ryland's land"![10]

Mr Thomas Ryland

TO ERDINGTON

Passing under Hunton Hill bridge with its three handsome arches and pierced piers, the line continues up the gradient of 1:95 to just past Fentham Road, where it slackens off to 1:330. Fentham Road is not marked on the original contract plan, but the bridge was built as part of the works for the line; along the whole five miles the only new bridges to have been built are at

Fentham Road bridge

Reservoir Road bridge—one of the two surviving original girder bridges.

Spaghetti Junction (several, however, have been altered). The land here belonged to Fentham's Charity, and the Aston Union Workhouse was shortly to be built on it, now Highcroft Hospital. At Reservoir Road (then called Queen's Head Road) the works involved raising the road level to pass over the girder bridge, and draining a large pool which lay between the railway and the Queen's Head Inn which then stood at the

Station Road, Erdington—the LMS Station sign is still visible on this 1983 photograph.

roadside on the corner of Gravelly Hill and Reservoir Road; the possibility of making a station here was considered. Summer Lane (the "Lane leading to Oscott") had to be lowered, and the three large brickyards between Summer Lane and Station Road (then Sheep Street) presented a problem. Not only was there compensation to pay, but the smoke and dirt from the kilns would be a nuisance to passengers.[11] This area, between the railway and the Post Office, was later a large goods yard, but the line as built may not have had even the simple siding that was there by 1886. The remains of the extensive goods yard could still be seen in 1982 (gone in 1983). The embankment from Summer Lane to Station Road is 18 feet at its highest point.

After passing under Wood End Lane and Moor End Lane (none of the other roads then existed) the Eastern Line would have been on the surface and level as it approached the Green, then the centre of the village.

Chester Road. The original girder bridge has been replaced. The road was lowered when the bridge was built, conveniently for modern buses! The coal wharf was just to the left of this photograph.

ERDINGTON STATION

Mr Burke thought that having a station on an embankment was inconvenient and expensive. Although there was housing on the western side, they were small houses not good enough for "Clerks and people living out of Birmingham"—"the majority of them are paupers I think".[12] Evidence was given at the enquiry that there were a large number of market gardens on the western side, and the station would be an advantage for them.[13] Development of the area between Gravelly Lane and the railway did not take place until the 1890s. In his report to the Board of Trade, the Inspector stated that the station was platforms only, and the fencing was incomplete. This was because the waiting rooms and ticket office, with their rustic wood panelling, were still under construction at the time, though no doubt ready for the autumn rains.

The eastern station would have been ideally placed, on the surface near the present swimming baths, "100 yards from the centre of the village".[14] The respectable people of Erdington lived on the eastern side, and building land was "Well-adapted for villas and houses of the first class".[15]

TO CHESTER ROAD

The steady climb continues, with a gradient of 1:107, the line being on a low embankment or on the surface. At Chester Road the Act required "a bridge of a clear width of 40 feet at the least, and a height of 16 feet for a width of 6 feet on either side of the centre of the arch, and the Company shall not lower the surface of the said turnpike road more than 3' 6" from its present level, and . . . drain the said turnpike road where the same is crossed by the railway". At the enquiry it was stated that this would be the lowest point for half a mile round; it was proposed to solve the drainage problem by a large sink pit.[16] The road was owned by the Stonall, Stonebridge, and Castle Bromwich Turnpike Trust, and the trustees favoured the Eastern Company; Machin, the Chairman, was pro-Western, but William Fowler got the pro-Eastern resolution passed when Machin was absent.[17]

The Eastern Line would have sloped gently down to Holly Lane, crossed by an overbridge,

'Berwood', Mr Wheelwright's villa residence

and up to Chester Road, where, although the line was in a 13 foot cutting the level of the road needed to be raised 5 feet. This was exactly the crossing point in the planned 1847 railway surveyed by Joseph Locke. The Bell and Cuckoo Inn stood where the two turnpike roads crossed, and the proprietress, Mary Fowler (no relation) also owned a villa on Chester Road near the proposed line. The line was designed to pass at an equal

Chester Road Station. Though opened eighteen months later, the buildings are to the same design as Wylde Green, and similar to Erdington except for the canopy. The roof overhangs to give nominal shelter from the rain, and the windows are shaped in the contemporary Gothic style. The details on these buildings are quite different from those on the Lichfield Extension line at Four Oaks and Blake Street, built twenty years later by the same company.

distance between her house and "one equally good if not better belonging to Mr Wheelwright"[18]— probably the houses later known as 'Berwood' and 'Holifast Grange', as there were no houses on the south side of Chester Road at the time, the orphanage still being a pipe-dream of Josiah Mason, not realised until 1869.

CHESTER ROAD STATION

Although both Companies' prospectuses mentioned a station at Chester Road, there were no details, and the present station with its early LNWR gothic buildings of rustic wood panels dates from 1st December 1863, one and a half years after the opening of the line. The siding on the south side of Chester Road was a coal wharf, but does not appear to date from 1862; the rapid increase in the

number of houses in the area shown by the 1871 census returns would have created sufficient demand from an early date, and it was a busy place within living memory. Its position on the east side of the line can still be seen, rising from road level to its junction with the track 200 yards to the south.

TO WYLDE GREEN

Considerable difficulties over the originally planned route forced the engineers to build the line at the extreme edge of the limits of deviation, with the demolition of Sheffields Farm which stood where the footbridge is now. This was done to avoid passing through the school playground (which would have meant the closing of Green Lanes School), and saved the expense of a bridge over Green Lanes by diverting it alongside the embankment. The land all belonged to the Warden and Society of Sutton, whose surveyor took the precaution of reporting on the effects of the line on their property on 14th January 1859, the main point being "it is manifestly impossible for the works to be executed and the School to retain its present position". At about this time the school log book refers to unidentified 'troubles' and their eventual solution—no doubt the building and opening of the railway were a worry and a distraction, and possibly there was some campaigning to be done for a footbridge in addition to the farm crossing at Sheffield Road. The original footbridge was wooden, and the Board of Trade Inspector made enquiries to ascertain that the road was only for farm access before giving his approval for the crossing gates (made of seasoned oak at a cost of £30) which were originally provided. Just before the post marking 3½ miles from Aston the line passes over another bridge, made so that the farmer could gain access to his fields. The summit of the line is near the 3¼ mile post, where the gradient changes from the gentle rise of 1:266 which commenced at the 3 mile post to a descent of 1:256, being on a slight embankment most of the way.

After passing under Chester Road, the Eastern Line would descend a 1:100 slope to pass under Penns Lane, up to 1:100 to near Brooks Road, and down 1:100 to Wylde Green. A station at Penns Lane was suggested, although this would still have been over a quarter of a mile from Baron

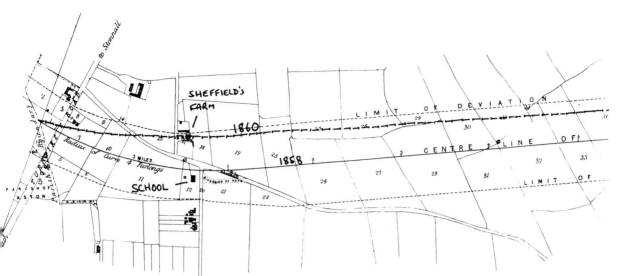

The line as originally planned. The course finally chosen was along the dotted 'limits of deviation' line through Sheffield's Farm.

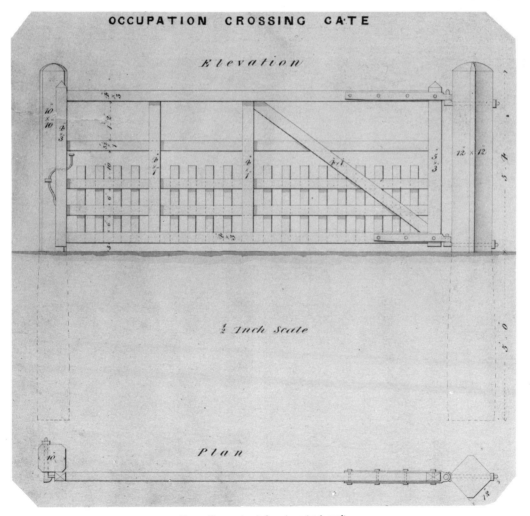

From the contract drawings (reduced)

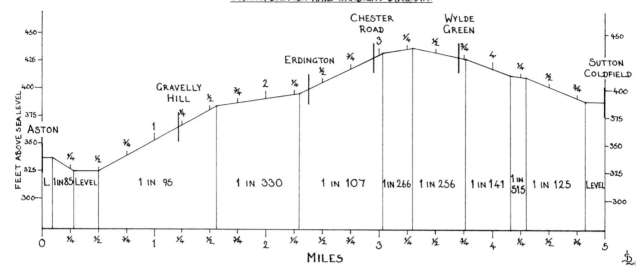

GRADIENTS
ASTON~ SUTTON COLDFIELD
FROM A BRITISH RAIL GRADIENT DIAGRAM.

Gradients, Aston—Sutton Coldfield. From a British Rail gradient diagram.

Webster's mill at Penns. Over most of the route the line would have been in a shallow cutting.

WYLDE GREEN STATION

Speculative building, or at least the sale of building land, appears to have been going on irrespective of the advent of the railway by the time of the Inquiry. John Smith was the owner of most of the land through which the line passed in the Wylde Green area, and he had laid out a new road in 1859. The LNWR decided that this new road would be a better site for their station than the projected Jockey Road one, and they may have hoped to serve the Chester Road area from this station as well, and constructed the station at Chester Road when it was realised that neither Wylde Green nor Erdington were satisfying the needs of that area. The new road immediately took the name Station Road, and it must have been a prominent landmark with its massive timbers supporting the waiting rooms, still to be seen from the car park, as are the fence-post sockets in the retaining wall.

At the time of the Inquiry, building in the area had been concentrated at the Boldmere crossroads,

Wylde Green Station, showing the massive supports to the booking office and the fence post sockets in the brickwork.

but instead of building the new church there the Rector chose a site some distance away at the top of the hill. This decision may have been speculative, in anticipation of a building boom on the coming of the railway, but another reason seems to have been to counteract the Roman Catholic influence of the Pugin church by the crossroads and the domination of the skyline by Oscott College and Erdington Abbey Church. At the Inquiry the whole district was spoken of as being potentially very prosperous (the Rector, incidentally, owned a great deal of land in the Boldmere area) and the people already living there were described: "a great many of them are clerks and small business men with salaries I suppose of £100 a year . . . who live in houses below the good class of villas. Where is their business? In Birmingham."[19]

The eastern station would have been in a cutting on the north side of Wylde Green Road, and was much criticised by the western party because of the steep hill to be negotiated up to the turnpike road (a height of 74 feet) and it was said to be too far away from the main area of population.[20]

The picturesque cutting and Driffold bridge.

TO SUTTON

The last 1¼ miles of the line are downhill, the slope increasing after Jockey Road to 1:125, becoming level at Brassington Avenue. Formidable earthworks were involved on this stretch, the line passing 25 feet below the Driffold and 18 feet below Manor Hill, the cutting at one point being 38 feet deep. This cutting destroyed parts of the remaining foundations of the medieval Manor House of Sutton—luckily they are described by Miss Bracken in her *Forest and Chase of Sutton Coldfield* published in 1860. Manor Road did not exist in 1860, but the dramatic bridge linking cutting to embankment was built in any case—within a few yards the line emerges from its deep cutting onto a 40-foot high embankment. This was a main source of objection to the line—"It is an embankment of nearly 50 feet high which goes across one of the most beautiful valleys in the Midland Counties and completely destroys a view which is quite unsurpassed—it is a most atrocious thing" (Baron Webster).[21] However, the Rector stated that the only people to have their view shut out were "of the class of small houses where you see tea-accommodation in the window."[22] The cutting involved excavating some 200,000 cubic yards, no doubt used to make the embankment across the valley,[23] and there was a complication at Jockey Road where the line had to be lowered by 5 feet from the originally planned level.

Manor Hill—an original girder bridge.

The bridge over Manor Road looking west—the embankment begins to the right.

The Eastern Line would have been level after crossing over Coles Lane, having descended a 1:100 incline from Wylde Green Road. Near

33

Ebrook Culvert

The 'Eastern' route across Maney Hill Road. 'A' is the site for Wylde Green Station.

where the line was to pass under Maney Hill Road stood Lower Maney Farm, the home of Captain F. Riland Bedford, owned by his brother the Rector. They petitioned against the line, saying it would interfere with their beautifully situated much-improved mansion; the surveyor, Burke, responded that it was merely a superior farmhouse and the line was in a 15—20 foot cutting there anyway. The local roads were said to be in a poor state, and would be improved on the line being built.[24] To cross under Upper Holland Road involved diverting it to the south, which was opposed by the owner of a huxter's shop at the bottom of the newly made Sadler Street (now Duke Street), as it would take away the advantage of the corner site. At the Inquiry the objection was not taken seriously, and as to the neighbouring cottagers, far from being inconvenienced, they "would be amused by looking at the train from the windows."[25]

SUTTON COLDFIELD STATION

The position of the terminus station is partly obscured by the work done for the later Lichfield extension, which necessitated building a second bridge over Park Road to the east and slightly lower than the 1860 one. The old station platforms and buildings were almost completely removed, and the track relaid in order to make the new station. The original station with its yard occupied what is now the car park, and was formed by

Site of the 1862 Sutton Station.

excavating on the Sutton side and embanking on the Park side; the resulting slopes were grassed over, the present retaining walls dating from 1884.[26] The position of the station was criticised as being expensive to make and awkward to approach, both from the town and the park. It was 42 feet above the level of the rival station, which was at the bottom of the valley, and 43 feet below the Three Tuns Inn, which was considered to be the centre of Sutton at the time; a good route for onward extension was available along the valley west of Anchorage Road (the Sutton Park line eventually blocked this route).[27] The original station was constructed with the main buildings (waiting room and booking office) and a canopy on the east platform, separated from the west platform by three lines of track, the near two being connected at the very end of the line to a turntable, so that the engine could uncouple from the train, turn on the turntable, and pass down the central line and couple on to the front of the train returning to Aston. There was a wooden footway across the lines to the west platform, as well as the safer access along the path past the end of the line; the west platform was referred to in the plans as the arrivals platform, but was probably only used

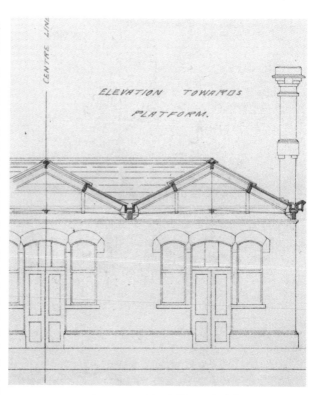

The 1862 Booking Office (reduced) from the contract drawings.

Sutton Coldfield Station c. 1870, with the added refreshment rooms in the foreground. The wagon turntable and dock are shown.

(Above) Carriage Trucks—early Grand Junction

(Below) The Great Western Railway version

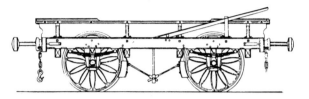

at busy times. A small wagon turntable on the line adjacent to the main platform gave access to a short siding at right angles to the line next to the refreshment room, and if this turntable was rotated through 45 degrees, there was a ramp for the end-loading of carriages onto carriage trucks, which could then be pulled into the siding to await the train. A facility for the owners of carriages to take their equipages with them on the train, with their horses in a horse-box truck, was provided at many of the more substantial stations. On the Railway Road side there were two sidings parallel to the platforms, one passing through a goods shed, connected to each other by wagon turntables, and there were two other sidings at an angle.

The Eastern Line would have terminated in Haywards Meadow, which was on the east side of the Parade between Newhall Street and South Parade (neither then existed). In its favour was the easy access to the turnpike road and the prospect of a future extension to Sutton Park for the excursion traffic. Against it was the steep climb up to the centre of the town, which was generally agreed to be the Three Tuns, the Parade being quite undeveloped until the 1880s; most excursionists going to the park apparently went up into the town first "to get beer".[28] At Haywards Meadow the turnpike road was on an embankment made in 1817 when the Mill Street hill was made less steep by making a shallow cutting at the top and raising the level of the approach at the bottom, and so the site had a reputation as a cold, damp spot,

"Sutton Park having a number of pools in it and considerable bogs a great accumulation of moisture arises in the valley—it is such a cold spot it is enough to give any Railway passengers the ague that go to a station there, at least I think so."[29]

Another objection related to the possibility of extending the line to Lichfield, when the best route would be to branch off near Coles Lane and, crossing Rectory Road, up past Four Oaks along the present Lichfield line; this would have relegated Sutton Station to a little branch of its own.

CONSTRUCTION

As to any incidents or problems in constructing the line, little is recorded. Eckersley and Reed's contract included 642,500 cubic yards of excavations, 503,100 cubic yards of embankments, at 5d per cubic yard, 16,543 cubic yards of brickwork, 5,207 cubic feet of creosoted Memel[30] timber, £2,057 for fences of "seasoned oak or slow-grown larch", £2,142 for iron girders, and £1,000 for Derbyshire stone, the total amount being £50,536 9s 3d. However, the LNWR supplied the permanent way, which consisted of 21-foot double-headed

Staffordshire brick and Derbyshire stone—details of bridge design at the Tame viaduct and at Highbridge Road.

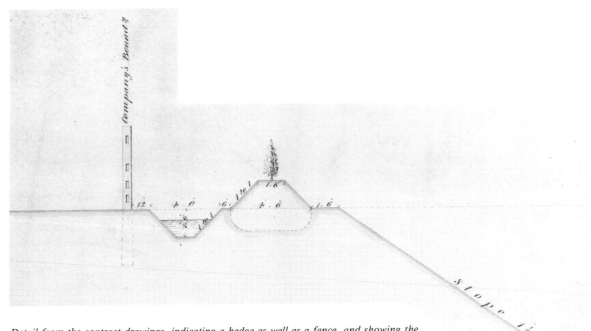

Detail from the contract drawings, indicating a hedge as well as a fence, and showing the current practice of covering the sleepers with ballast.

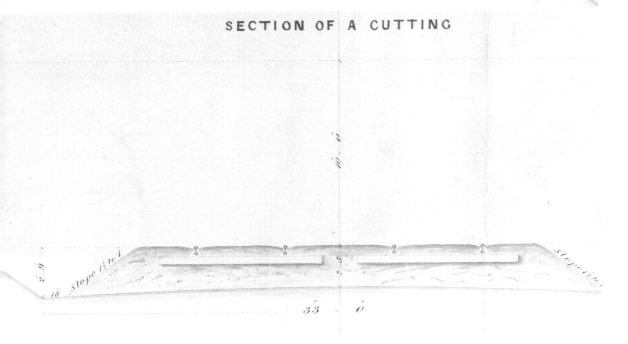

SECTION OF A CUTTING

rails weighing 84 lbs per yard, set in cast iron chairs secured by oak keys, each chair being fastened to the sleepers by two treenails and an iron spike. The sleepers rested on ballast 18 inches deep, which was laid to cover the sleepers and leave only part of the rail above ground; the bed on which the ballast was laid was 33 feet wide.[31] Eckersley and Reed's contract included £2,659 18s for laying the track, but did not include the station at Sutton, which was let separately to the firm of Charles Burkett of Wolverhampton, and not started until January 1862.

Some of the men involved in the construction of the line are listed in the 1861 census return for Sutton—Elisha Perigo, railway inspector, was staying at the Horse and Jockey, George Smith had a house in High Street, and was a railway contractor, and a timekeeper, Joseph Ashurst, lived at Doe Bank. In various lodging houses, cottages, outbuildings, and private houses there were 63 railway labourers and excavators, 23 of them born in Ireland, and others from 20 different English counties. Almost all of them lived near the centre of the town, Halfway House and 'Near Rectory' being the most distant addresses. Most of them were single men in their twenties but there were some family men and a few over fifty years old. Ten years later, there were twelve railway employees, including the station-masters of Chester Road and Wylde Green, three porters, three clerks, two platelayers, a guard, and the refreshment room manageress and waitress; the Sutton Coldfield station-master is not listed.

The line was inspected on 28th May 1862 by Lieutenant Colonel William Yolland, according to the rules of the Board of Trade for all new lines. He had been active in preparing early editions of the Ordnance Survey maps, and served on many accident enquiries, including the Tay Bridge disaster in 1880. He described the line briefly, mentioning 10 bridges carrying the line over roads, 4 of girders and 6 with brick arches, and 8 carrying roads over the railway, 3 with girders, 5 with brick arches, and the viaducts over the river and the canal; these are all still to be seen (some subject to alteration), except that the underbridges at Sheffield Road allotments and near the canal are usually over-looked by modern travellers. Some of them, as at Hunton Hill, Driffold, and Manor Road, are handsome examples of railway architecture. Colonel Yolland commented that "the lever handles for the distant signals require to be brought together close to the station signals at some stations, and the facing points require indicators." It was due to pressure from the Board of Trade that the LNWR introduced the block system of signalling a few years later, involving the construction of signal boxes, the one at Sutton having to be demolished in 1884 for the new station —it stood a few yards to the south of the Park Road bridge. He reported that the line was unsafe for passenger traffic because the fences were unfinished, there were no clocks at the stations, the signalling needed adjustments, Gravelly Hill

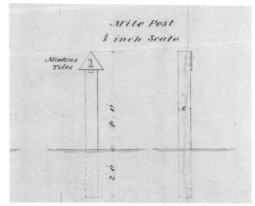

Line-side furniture. The original mile posts with their Minton tiles are long since gone, but there are ones as illustrated every ¼ mile on the down side, including a 5 mile post on platform 2 at Sutton; the only gradient post I have seen is on the down side just south of Erdington Station—not original!

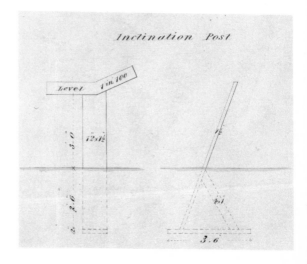

Handsome bridge at the Driffold

Humble cattle-arch by the canal

Station needed catch points, and the pillars at Sutton Station were too near the edge of the platform.

By the time the line was opened on 2nd June it had probably exceeded Errington's estimate of £70,000 which he had given at the Inquiry, where only 410,000 cubic yards of excavation were envisaged; the land was expected to cost £14,500 and the permanent way £19,400,[32] and these, together with the main Eckersley and Reed contract, brought the costs up to around £90,000. This is remarkably close to the estimate given at the Inquiry by James Burke of £87,400, in comparing it with the projected cost of the Eastern Line of £60,000; this was made up of £20,000 for land and £40,000 for construction.[33]

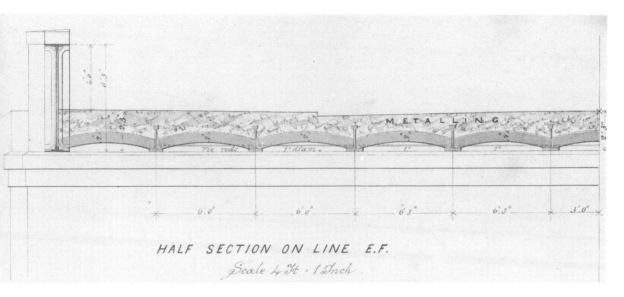

Design for a girder bridge, with brick vaulting. Although this is taken from the plan of a bridge on the Lichfield Extension Railway (not built), the girder bridges on the Sutton Branch are similar.

CHAPTER THREE

Early Days

THE OPENING

Most of the comment on the opening of the line was on its likely use by trippers to Sutton Park. The *Birmingham Daily Post* of 3rd June 1862 reported:

OPENING OF THE SUTTON COLDFIELD BRANCH RAILWAY YESTERDAY

Yesterday morning the new branch line, constructed from this town to the picturesque locality of Sutton Coldfield was opened for passenger traffic. Though the day was beautifully fine, and though several trains had been publicly announced to run during the forenoon and the earlier portion of the afternoon, comparatively few people took advantage of the opportunity of enjoying a refreshing trip into a neighbourhood which is replete with natural beauty. We should say that not more than a couple of thousand excursionists left the New Street Station, and we can only infer from this circumstance that the exquisite prospect around Sutton must be very little known by the inhabitants of Birmingham. One of the advantages of the new line will, however, be that it will afford to the community in this town a facility of devoting their leisure to the enjoyment of scenery the equal of which is not to be met with in the midland counties. The demesne appertaining to the manor of Sutton Coldfield comprises several thousand acres of richly-wooded land, and in it many thousands of excursionists may disperse themselves in parties without apprehension of intruding upon one another. They may luxuriate under greenwood shades to their heart's content, and on every hand will they meet something which will gratify the eye and elevate their ideas above the ordinary level of mental reflection. Without enlarging, however, on this subject, though it is prolific with interest, we will content ourselves with cordially recommending a visit to Sutton Park.

The arrival of the first passenger train over the new line was yesterday morning greeted by a large concourse of people, and though there was no external demonstrations of satisfaction, it was evident in the countenances of all assembled that the event was regarded as a "great fact." In the town there were no manifestations of rejoicing, such as have been usual on similar occasions in other places, but the gratification expressed by everybody one met was unequivocal and sincere. Towards the afternoon Sutton looked quite animated, the visitors who had come in by train flowing up the generally quiet streets in continuous streams in the direction of the Park, and foreshadowing what may be expected when the long-secluded beauty of the locality becomes fully known.

Aris's Birmingham Gazette for the same day carried a more enthusiastic and lyrical report:

OPENING OF THE BRANCH LINE TO SUTTON COLDFIELD.

Yesterday morning the branch line of the London and North-Western Railway from Aston to Sutton Coldfield was opened for passenger and luggage traffic. Hitherto the only means of conveyance to Sutton Coldfield from Birmingham that came within the reach of the general public has been the line of omnibuses, which have, after all, carried the passengers well and cheaply; but still that very numerous class of the community who have in the whole week only one half-day in which they can leave the busy town for rural haunts, found their brief time of relaxation much encroached upon when they went to visit the old park and "listen to the moaning of the woods," by the time necessarily occupied by the transit to and fro. Now all this is altered; the distance is reduced to half an hour each way; and, what is not a little thing, the cost of the journey is reduced by one-half. On Saturdays, Sundays, and Mondays in summer time there have always been a large number of visitors from Birmingham to Sutton Coldfield, pic-nic parties have been held beneath the shade of the green trees, and many a hard-handed artizan has had his heart gladdened, and has cast off some of the "carking cares" of the week, while wandering through the woods and by the pools of the Royal Chase, by the glimpses of the sylvan beauty around him. Nowhere else near Birmingham can the wearied citizen so fully and so freely luxuriate in the presence of the charms of nature; and now that it costs little money and little time to reach it, the enjoyment cannot fail to become more general. Good evidence of this is given in the large number of Birmingham people who visited Sutton Coldfield yesterday, and who, after wandering through the quiet old town, found their way to the Park. And not only is the place pleasant when one arrives there, but the journey by rail is pleasant too. The line is smooth and easy, and passes through a number of cuttings, the slopes of which are even now beginning to be covered by vegetation, very pleasant to the eye. Between the cuttings may be seen from the trains many a wide expanse of rural scenery, that is lost only too soon, but cannot be soon forgotten. The stations on the route, although not yet complete, seem to be placed at the most picturesque points on the line, and are themselves pretty buildings; and the carriages are new, airy, roomy, and comfortable. As the first train passed along the line yesterday morning, a little crowd had assembled at every point where it could be seen, and cheered heartily as it passed. Old men who saw it became garrulous in their narratives of the past, and prophesied that "Old Sutton" would now become "New Sutton;" practical hard-headed men began to speculate on the amount of money that it would bring into the town; and young men rejoiced in the anticipation that the air of quiet that hung about the place, and had stopped so many boisterous manifestations of fun, would exist no longer. At the terminus a large number of persons—amongst whom were Mr. J. Wright, the warden of Sutton Coldfield, Mr. Holbeche and Mr. Addenbrooke, deputy stewards; Messrs. Chavasse, Shaw, Smith, Brentnall, Tyler, and Wallace—had assembled to welcome the train, and many bashful passengers were quite overcome by their feelings at finding they had become for the nonce objects of great interest to the inhabitants of the town. Later in the day other trains came in bringing their quota of visitors, by far the largest number of whom arrived by the special excursion train at three o'clock. In this train there were no fewer than fifteen carriages, all of which were crowded with holiday people who had been tempted by the warm summer's day to leave Birming-ham for a country jaunt.

In the course of the day no fewer than 2,000 persons could have come by the different trains. The names of the officers connected with the line are—Mr. Angell, the company's engineer; Mr. Acaster, the contractors' engineer; Mr. Perrigo, the contractor's inspector; Mr. Tait, the contractors' foreman; and Mr. Gillson, the assistant engineer.

The leader writer for the *Birmingham Journal* of 31st May 1862 hinted at the future commuter traffic:

The completion of the railway between Birmingham and Sutton Coldfield deserves a passing word of comment and congratulation. Shareholders, engineers, and contractors have finished their part of the business satisfactorily, and all that is now wanted is the formal sanction of the Board of Trade to the opening of the line. When this event has taken place the rush of pleasure seekers will begin, and thousands of our townsmen will be glad to find in Sutton Park the fresh air and recreation they cannot easily obtain nearer home. We may perhaps venture to give a friendly hint both to our townsmen and our Sutton neighbours. We would have the former remember that as they obtain access to Sutton Park only out of neighbourly courtesy, it is the more incumbent upon them to see that no damage is done, and that the privilege is not in any way abused. On the other hand, the corporation of Sutton will no doubt act in a liberal spirit in framing such regulations as may be thought necessary—bearing in mind that the fewer and simpler the rules laid down, the more likely are they to meet with willing obedience. Rightly used, the opening of this railway ought to prove of great benefit to both towns, for many Birmingham men would be glad to take up their residence in Sutton, and the latter place will have a cheap and easy means of communication with Birmingham, which has hitherto been practically as far off from them as Rugby is from ourselves.

This leader was provoked by an article on another page of the same paper:

THE NEW BRANCH RAILWAY TO SUTTON COLDFIELD.

—On Wednesday last Colonel Yolland, of the Board of Trade Department of the Government, inspected the new branch line of railway to Sutton Coldfield, and in so doing was accompanied by gentlemen interested in the undertaking. The line runs through a beautiful neighbourhood, and is five miles in length. A good deal of labour has been involved in its construction, as may be judged from the fact that 700,000 cubic yards of material have been excavated. The brickwork is to the extent of about 23,000 cubic yards. The cost of the line will amount to £60,000. The line has occupied nineteen months in making, the works being executed under the direction of Mr. Acaster, engineer to the contractors, who were represented by Mr. Eckersley (firm of Eckersley and Read, of Manchester); and Mr. Angell, the resident engineer of the London and North-Western Line, has acted as Superintendent. Mr. Burkitt, builder, of Wolverhampton, has executed the work at the stations. Colonel Yolland expressed himself satisfied with the manner in which the line has been made, and, subject to some additions and modifications which he suggested, he will report favourably upon it to the Board of Trade. The result of the inspection, however, will not be officially notified for four or five days. Hopes are entertained that the line may be opened for traffic on Monday next. It is stated that the inhabitants of Sutton contemplate celebrating the event of the opening—an event so important to their local interests—by a public demonstration of some kind, and that it will most probably assume the time-honoured form of a banquet.

The banquet was duly provided, and fully reported in *Aris's Birmingham Gazette* for 3rd June; the Warden, Mr Josiah Wright, was in the Chair, W. S. Perkins was Vice-Chairman. After some solid speeches toasting the army and the church,

The CHAIRMAN said that he had now a long toast to propose, and what was worse still, he saw before him no one with whom he could identify it. The first part of it was, the Directors of the London and North-Western Railway Company, and he felt that they would all agree with him when he said that they owed a deep debt of gratitude to those gentlemen. He supposed that what had been done was a simple act of kindness on the part of those gentlemen, for they had not asked whether the line would pay, but only whether it would benefit "Old Sutton"—(laughter). They had not asked whether their money would be repaid, but only if the spending of it would do good, and they had made them a most admirable line. The directors had, no doubt, thought that the little town might one day become a great town, and in the meantime had determined to educate it by placing it in close proximity with the magnificent town of Birmingham. But they had not only to be grateful to the London and North-Western Railway Company, but to the shareholders of the line. The next part of the toast was, "and success to the Birmingham and Sutton Coldfield Branch," and that was doubtless what they would most enthusiastically drink—(applause). He hoped that the town would be improved in every way by the line of railway. He believed that it would be so, and he was sorry that they had not more enthusiastically received the first train. Now it was curious to think that on the first occasion the line had been used it had been to bring a director to marry a wife from Sutton Coldfield—(laughter). Of course he was not in a position to offer for any young ladies—the offer must come from the other side; but he hoped the good example would be followed—(renewed laughter). He had often heard one of the shareholders of the new line, Mr. Holbeche, speak of the difficulties he had had in getting up to town thirty years ago, but all that was altered now, and if it was only that they would be able to get up to town without much trouble he thought they ought to be thankful that they had got a railway. He had great pleasure in proposing the toast—(applause).

Mr. HOLBECHE, in responding, said he believed the branch of railway which had that day been opened would do more for the parish of Sutton Coldfield than any improvement that had been effected within his memory. He had lived within the parish for more than half a century, and he believed that no town had undergone a greater change within that time than had Sutton Coldfield—(Cries of "No, no," from Mr. Fielding). He remembered when the roads to Birmingham were impassable, when the roads to Walsall were impassable, and when to get to Coleshill they had to go a round of many miles—now all these places were within seven miles by railway. He had heard it said jokingly some thirty years ago, that they would ultimately become united with Birmingham, and now he was glad to see that they were very closely united with Birmingham. Already the prices of land had increased. It was not many years ago, since some land in Chester Road was sold for little more than £20. an acre, when they got better roads the price went up to £100. an acre, and now there was a railway more than £300. an acre was asked for it.

Mr. FIELDING, who also responded, said he had said " no, no," to Mr. Holbeche because he believed that within the last fifty years there had been a greater change in Birmingham than Sutton Coldfield. He was glad to feel that there was now a different feeling from that which had once existed between himself and the Corporation of Sutton Coldfield. He hoped the Corporation was at last going ahead, and he would say that when the Corporation was thrown open he would gladly be one of them, but he would not be a self-elected man.

Mr. ADDENBROOKE then sang " Viva Victoria."

Mr. THOMAS LLOYD next proposed " The Trade and Society of Sutton Coldfield." He said that he could not propose this toast without referring to a dear friend they had often seen there, the late Baron Webster, who was one of those men who, without any very brilliant parts, by his honesty, worth, and courtesy, found his way to the warmest place in their hearts. Mr. Webster had been the warden of Sutton Coldfield for many years, and he trusted that in proposing that toast he was not wrong in calling attention to his memory, and paying a tribute to his great worth. It was somewhat strange that a member of the upstart Corporation of Birmingham should be allowed the honour of proposing the toast that had been intrusted to him. To-day the Corporation of Sutton Coldfield was a happy Corporation, for they had nothing to do but spend money, and had no difficulty in collecting it. They had no tax-payers, or collectors with little books; one, two, three a summons and a warrant, but had ample funds with which they supported the widow, educated the child, and what was even more, pensioned the maiden. He was very glad that Birmingham was at last connected with this beautiful country, and he trusted that the inhabitants of Sutton Coldfield would never have reason to regret the connection. He was glad, he said, that the girls from Birmingham would have the opportunity of walking beneath the serene shades of Sutton woods, and that the young men could there make love to them —(applause). In conclusion he wished all prosperity to the ancient and honourable corporation.

After a song from Mr. SMITH,

The CHAIRMAN said that he would only respond for himself, and that for his part he felt excessively obliged for the manner

in which they had received his health. He was glad to hear, on the authority of an excellent judge, that they were at last going ahead a little at Sutton Coldfield. He hoped that the town would derive some benefit from its connection with Birmingham, but that at the same time some of its pleasant characteristics would not be lost in the spread of improvement.

Dr. BODDINGTON, in responding, said he hoped the Birmingham people would not come there to build tall chimneys, but to inhabit pleasant houses, gardens, and fields, and to take the benefit of the park in getting a good, healthy circulation and breathing.

Mr. WILKINS also responded, and expressed himself willing to see even tall chimneys, so that the material prosperity of the town was increased.

The VICE-CHAIRMAN said he had great pleasure in proposing the next toast, " The health of the Contractors, Messrs. Eckersley and Read." He was not personally acquainted with either of the gentlemen, but he felt satisfied that every one present wished to be conveyed to them their sincere thanks for the substantial manner in which they had executed the works entrusted to them. He hoped that in the course of a few years they would have the happiness of seeing Messrs. Eckersley and Read amongst them as the contractors for an extension of the line to Lichfield.

Mr. ECKERSLEY said he had to return thanks on the behalf of his partner and himself, for the kind manner in which their names had been proposed and received. To quote Scripture, it might on this occasion be said that " their lines had fallen in pleasant places," and he only feared that they would not have the pleasure of meeting them again on any extension of the line, as it was very seldom that the same contractor carried out two lines in conjunction. Although, as the Irish saying went, he said it who ought not to say it, he believed that the new line had been substantially carried out. The inspector had done them the honour to say that the works were very good, and he would say that the road was in excellent order, so that they could travel at any speed with safety. He might be allowed to say that contractors were exceptions from the old adage that ' rolling stones gather no moss," inasmuch as they were of necessity rolling stones, and gathered what moss they could on the way. In conclusion, he again begged to thank them for the kind manner in which the health of himself and his partner had been drunk.

" The Ladies," and other toasts followed.

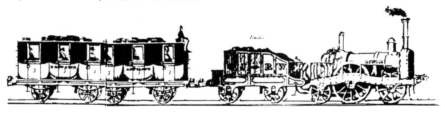

THE PASSENGERS

On the expectation of holiday traffic, a company was formed to build and operate a fashionable hotel. Most of the promoters of the Sutton Royal Hotel Company Limited—Payn, Lucy, Elwell, Gwyther, Chavasse—had been directors of one of the rival railway companies; however, financial problems caused them to liquidate in 1866, and the grandiose building never

seems to have been a going concern as a hotel. Although the excursion and holiday traffic was important, it must have been clear very soon that commuters would form the backbone of the passenger service. Time-tables for 1862 and 1870 show how the service settled down to reflecting the familiar rush-hour patterns of today:

LONDON AND NORTH-WESTERN RAILWAY.

SUTTON COLDFIELD BRANCH.

THE BRANCH LINE of RAILWAY between ASTON and SUTTON COLDFIELD will be OPENED for GOODS and PASSENGER TRAFFIC on the 2nd day of JUNE, 1862, when the

FOLLOWING TIME TABLE FOR JUNE, 1862,

WILL COME INTO OPERATION :—

DOWN TRAINS.

ORDINARY FARES TO AND FROM SUTTON.			STATIONS.	WEEK DAYS							SUNDAYS.		
1st class.	2nd class.	3rd class.	Classes between Birmingham and Sutton	1, 2, 3 class.	1, 2, 3 class.	1, 2, 3 class.	1, 2, 3 class.	1, 2, 3 class.	1, 2, 3 class.	1, 2, 3 class.	1, 2, 3 class.	1, 2, 3 class.	1, 2, 3 class.
s. d.	s. d.	s. d.	Leave										
20 9	15 6	9 10	LONDON (Euston)	...	...	6 15	9 0	11 15	...	5 0	...	10 0	...
...	...	...	Leamington	...	...	8 10	10 50	1 10	...	7 5	...	12 30	...
...	...	...	Coventry	...	...	9 5	12 5	1 45	...	7 40	...	1 5	...
...	...	...	Liverpool	4 5	...	...	9 0	11 30	1 15	5 0	4 5	9 30	...
...	...	...	Manchester	...	...	...	9 30	12 0	1 45	5 15	...	9 20	...
...	...	...	Chester	4 35	...	...	9 0	12 10	...	5 25	4 35	10 0	...
...	...	...	Stafford	6 20	...	8 0	11 15	1 48	4 25	7 15	6 20	12 10	...
2 9	2 0	1 5	Wolverhampton	7 0	7 10	8 45	11 50	2 30	5 30	7 45	6 55	12 55	...
2 3	1 6	1 1	Dudley Port	7 10	7 27	8 57	12 5	2 50	5 40	7 55	7 12	1 9	...
1 9	1 6	0 11½	Oldbury	...	7 34	9 3	...	2 57	5 18	8 1	7 19	1 15	...
1 6	1 3	0 10	Smethwick	7 18	7 42	9 9	12 15	3 5	5 48	8 7	7 27	1 21	...
1 9	1 3	0 11	Walsall	6 45	7 45	9 15	12 10	3 25	5 40	7 50	6 30	12 45	5 30
2 0	1 6	1 0	Wednesbury	6 53	...	8 18	11 8	2 18	5 23	7 13	6 38	12 53	...
2 3	1 6	1 0½	Great Bridge	6 58	...	8 23	11 4	2 23	5 19	7 9	7 43	12 58	...
2 3	1 6	1 1	Dudley	7 0	...	8 40	11 55	2 40	5 10	7 50	7 5	12 0	...
...	...	...	Willenhall	...	7 43	9 8	...	2 8	5 38	...	...	...	...
1 3	1 0	0 6½	Perry Barr	...	8 11	9 33	12 25	2 36	6 6	8 4	...	...	5 45
				a.m.	a.m.	a.m.	p.m.	p.m.	p.m.	p.m.			
1 0	0 9	0 6½	BIRMINGHAM	7 40	8 50	10 10	1 10	3 45	6 5	8 20	8 45	2 30	7 30
			Arrive at										
0 10	0 7	0 5	ASTON	7 47	8 57	10 17	1 17	3 52	6 12	8 27	8 52	2 37	7 37
0 8	0 5	0 3½	GRAVELLY HILL	7 51	9 1	10 21	1 21	3 56	6 16	8 31	8 56	2 41	7 41
0 6	0 4	0 2½	ERDINGTON	7 54	9 4	10 24	1 24	3 59	6 19	8 34	8 59	2 44	7 44
0 4	0 3	0 1	WYLD GREEN	7 59	9 9	10 29	1 29	4 4	6 24	8 39	9 4	2 49	7 49
...	...	...	SUTTON COLDFIELD	8 5	9 15	10 35	1 35	4 10	6 30	8 45	9 10	2 55	7 55

UP TRAINS.

Return Fares from or to SUTTON.		STATIONS.	WEEK DAYS.								SUNDAYS.		
1st class.	2nd class.	Classes between Sutton and Birmingham.	1, 2, 3 class.	1, 2, 3 class.	1, 2, 3 class.	1, 2, 3 class.	1, 2, 3 class.	1, 2, 3 class.	1, 2, 3 class.	1, 2, 3 class.	1, 2, 3 class.	1, 2, 3 class.
s. d.	s. d.	Leave	a.m.	a.m.	a.m.	p.m.	p.m.	p.m.	p.m.	a.m.	p.m.	p.m.
0 6	0 4	SUTTON COLDFIELD	8 15	9 30	10 50	2 25	4 30	6 55	9 0	9 30	3 15	8 30
0 9	0 6	WYLD GREEN	8 19	9 34	10 54	2 29	4 34	6 59	9 4	9 34	3 19	8 34
1 0	0 8	ERDINGTON	8 23	9 38	10 58	2 33	4 38	7 3	9 8	9 38	3 24	8 38
1 3	1 0	GRAVELLY HILL	8 26	9 41	11 1	2 36	4 41	7 6	9 11	9 41	3 26	8 41
		ASTON	8 30	9 45	11 5	2 40	4 45	7 10	9 15	9 45	3 30	8 45
		Arrive at										
1 6	1 3	BIRMINGHAM	8 40	9 55	11 15	2 50	4 55	7 20	9 25	9 55	3 40	8 55
2 0	1 6	Perry Bar	9 45	10 45	12 35	2 45	5 10	8 5	9 30	...	6 0	8 55
...	...	Willenhall	10 13	11 12	1 2	3 12	6 7	...	9 57	...	6 27	...
3 3	2 6	Dudley	9 40	10 50	11 45	3 30	5 25	8 10	10 15	11 10	7 0	9 30
3 3	2 3	Great Bridge	9 49	11 31	12 31	3 49	6 44	8 9	...	...	6 48	9 38
3 0	2 3	Wednesbury	9 53	11 8	12 38	3 53	6 48	8 13	10 34	...	6 43	9 33
2 9	2 0	Walsall	10 5	11 15	12 50	3 10	5 25	8 25	10 0	...	6 30	9 15
2 3	2 0	Smethwick	8 55	10 19	11 44	3 10	5 10	7 40	9 44	10 44	...	9 11
2 9	2 3	Oldbury	9 22	10 27	11 52	3 15	5 37	8 18	9 52	10 52	...	9 19
3 3	2 6	Dudley Port	9 4	10 36	11 34	3 20	5 19	7 49	10 2	11 1	...	9 23
4 3	3 3	Wolverhampton	9 20	11 0	11 47	4 25	5 30	8 0	10 20	11 1	...	9 23
...	...	Stafford	9 48	11 40	12 15	...	6 10	8 30	11 23	1 25	...	10 25
...	...	Chester	11 35	...	2 0	...	8 7	10 5	2 15	4 10	...	11 25
...	...	Manchester	12 0	2 45	2 5	...	8 0	10 15	2 45	4 45	...	2 15
...	...	Liverpool	12 10	3 5	2 30	...	8 35	10 45	3 15	1 50	...	5 15
...	...	Coventry	10 4	11 27	12 33	4 5	6 18	8 14	...	...	...	...
...	...	Leamington	10 35	12 0	...	4 45	6 45	8 55	...	...	...	...
...	...	LONDON (Euston)	1 30	...	3 30	7 0	...	11 0	...	6 15	...	...

TIME TABLES FOR FEBRUARY, 1870.

SUTTON COLDFIELD TO BIRMINGHAM.

UP	WEEK DAYS																			SUNDAYS			
	1 2 3	1 2 3	1 2 3	1 2 3	1 2 3	1 2 3	1 2 3	1 2 3	1 2 3	1 2 3	Gov	1 2 3	1 2 3	1 2 3	1 2 3	1 2 3	1 2 3	1 2 3		1 2 3	1 2 3	1 2 3	Gov 1 2 3
Sutton Coldfield	6 50	8 0	8 30	8 36	9 25	1045	1145	1240	2 20	2 30	2 55	5 0	5 50	6 45	8 25	1020	9 50	1 50		5 35	9 15		
Wylde Green	6 54	8 3		8 39	9 29	1049	1149	1244		2 33	2 59	5 4	5 54	6 49	8 29	1024	9 54	1 54		5 38	9 19		
Chester Road	6 57	8 7	8 35		9 32	1052	1152	1247	2 25		3 2	5 7	5 57	6 52	8 32	1027	9 57	1 57		5 41	9 22		
Erdington	7 1	8 11		8 42	9 36	1056	1155	1251		2 37	3 5	5 11	6 1	6 56	8 37	1031	10 1	2 1		5 44	9 26		
Gravelly Hill	7 4	8 14	8 40		9 39	1059	1158	1254	2 30		3 8	5 14	6 4	7 0	8 40	1035	10 4	2 4		5 47	9 29		
Aston	7 8	8 18		8 49	9 43	11 3	12 2	1258		2 43	3 12	5 18	6 8	7 4	8 44	1039	10 8	2 8		5 51	9 23		
Vauxhall					9 47		12 6			3 16	5 22			7 8			1012	2 12		5 55	9 37		
Birmingham	7 20	8 30	8 53	9 0	9 55	1115	1215	1 10	2 43	2 53	3 26	5 35	6 20	7 18	8 55	1053	1020	2 20		6 5	9 47		

BIRMINGHAM TO SUTTON COLDFIELD.

DOWN	1 2 3	1 2 3	Gov	1 2 3	1 2 3	1 2 3	1 2 3	1 2 3	1 2 3	1 2 3	1 2 3	1 2 3	1 2 3	1 2 3	1 2 3	1 2 3	Gov	1 2 3	1 2 3	1 2 3
Birmingham	7 15	8 40	10 0	11 0	11 40	12 0	1 5	1 15	2 15	4 5	5 15	6 15	6 35	7 40	9 15	11 5		9 5	1 15	2 35 8 35
Vauxhall		8 45	10 8	11 5			2 21	4 10			7 45						9 10	1 20	2 43 8 40	
Aston	7 22	8 49	1012	11 9	12 7		1 22	2 23	4 14	5 22		6 42	7 49	9 22	1112		9 14	1 24	2 47 8 44	
Gravelly Hill	7 26	8 53	1016	1113	1211	1 15		2 27	4 18	5 26	6 25		7 53	9 26	1116		9 18	1 28	2 51 8 48	
Erdington	7 29	8 56	1019	1116	1214		1 28	2 32	4 21	5 29		6 48	7 56	9 29	1119		9 21	1 31	2 54 8 51	
Chester Road	7 33	9 0	1023	1119	1218	1 20		2 36	4 25	5 33	6 30		8 0	9 33	1123		9 25	1 35	2 58 8 55	
Wylde Green	7 37	9 4	1027	1123	1222		1 32	2 44	4 39	5 37		6 52	8 4	9 37	1127		9 29	1 39	3 2 8 59	
Sutton Coldfield	7 43	9 10	1033	1229	1228	1 28	1 38	2 46	4 35	5 43	6 38	6 58	8 10	9 43	1133		9 35	1 45	3 8 9 5	

Original Royal Hotel was opened May 1865
(later a Sanitorium and now Municipal Offices)

44

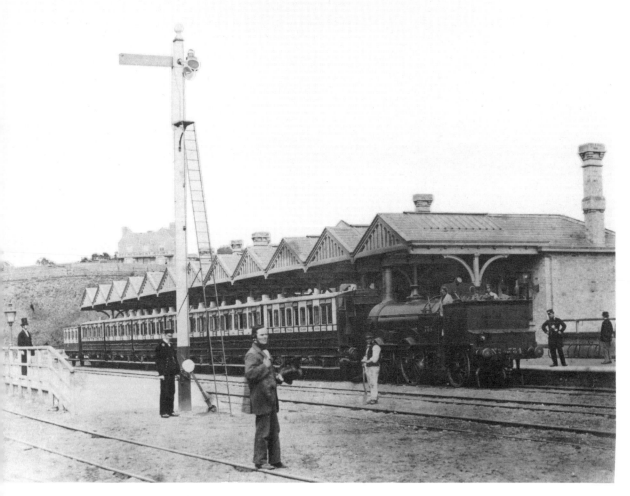

An early photograph of Sutton Station; the lack of refreshment rooms and the absence of the 'Royal Hotel' in the background, indicate an early date, 1862 or 1863.

THE TRAINS

The photograph illustrates the type of train which made the regular journey to and from Sutton. A McConnell 'M' class 0-4-2 tank engine draws a set of six four-wheeled coaches, the two end ones being 3rd class with brakes, the four centre ones composite 1st/2nd class; the train is completed by a single carriage of an older type. The signals and points are operated by adjacent levers—the signal shown is at danger, at 45 degrees it would indicate caution, and the vertical position would be all clear. Information about the early trains is scarce, but there is nothing to indicate that they ran less smoothly and easily than anticipated.

THE JOURNEY

This is described in *Sutton Coldfield, a history and guide* by Eliezer Edwards, 1880 (a present-day account would have different features to describe!):

CHAPTER II.

THE JOURNEY TO SUTTON.

———

"The massive engine stood in front, and fiery red it shone,
And spat forth hissing steam, as if impatient to be gone ;
One minute more, and like a ship just launched into the main
With unimpeded easy march, majestic moved the train."

———

New Street Station resounds suddenly with the shriek from the engine of our train as we move slowly towards the tunnel, dash into the darkness, and rush down the steep incline to pass under the girder bridge which carries the Great Western Railway. From this point we begin to rise until we get to level ground again near the ticket platform at Banbury Street. The Proof-house discharges a volley as we pass. We throw a hasty glance at the busy goods yard at Duddeston Row, and at the lofty stone building which was the Queen's Hotel, when the low shed near it was the terminus of the London and Birmingham Railway. We rattle across the wilderness of rails where the various lines diverge, and soon approach our first stopping place—Vauxhall. As we slacken speed and look out upon the left we see a clock on the west front of a building. That plain brick structure was the booking office, forty years ago, when this was the Birmingham terminus of the Grand Junction Railway from Liverpool and Manchester. There the writer, in the year 1837, took his first railway ticket, and made acquaintance with a mode of travelling which was as strange to him then as a trip in a balloon would be now.

We rattle on again and are soon at Aston. The old Hall stands on the hill top, as it has for three hundred years, but the town has crept up to it, and the avenue of trees, which at one time reached down to the railway embankment and even beyond it, has been replaced by populous streets. The fine spire of the Old Church rises above the tree tops by the river Tame. Away to our right, on the top of a hill, we see a large building crowned by a tower and spire. That is the Aston Union Poorhouse, and although it is now so much to our right, the curve is so great that when we next stop it will be half-a-mile to our left. Those large pools on the right are the Corporation water works reservoirs, and the massive square buildings just beyond, are the sheds for the colossal engines which pump the water to the reservoir near Monument Lane, Edgbaston, four miles away, and at a higher level by two hundred and thirty five feet. We soon reach Gravelly Hill Station, the only one on this line in a cutting, all the others being upon high embankments. The station yard is prettily planted with flowers and shrubs. Our next stopping place is Erdington, and as we approach it, we see the square tower of the Church among the trees. The Station is nearly opposite the Roman Catholic Church, which is one of Pugin's very finest works, the spire being remarkably beautiful. On the left we see the great Catholic College at Oscott, crowning a fir-clothed hill. The next Station adjoins the Chester Road, the old highway from London to that City, and thence to Ireland. It was

busy once with coaches and posting, but is now comparatively deserted. On our right we see the lofty tower of Sir Josiah Mason's Orphanage, and if we are lucky as to time, we may, as we stay, catch the sound of the clock chimes, the most musical in this part of the country. The institution is a most noble one. Hundreds of fatherless children are housed, clothed, educated, and otherwise well cared for within its walls, entirely by the self-sacrificing munificence of one man, whose bounty has so enriched it, that its provisions will be available for the benefit of generation after generation of orphans, for ever.

The next stopping-place is Wylde Green, where we give up our tickets. On an eminence to our left is the pretty church of Boldmere. A little to the right of the church we get a glimpse of one of the large pools or lakes of Sutton Park—Powell's Pool. Beyond is the far-famed group of trees known as Barr Beacon, standing on a lofty hill, whose summit has often shown the ruddy glare of the signal of danger, but at no time with a fiercer glow than when the Spanish Armada came in sight of England's western shores. Then from one end of the country to the other, hill answered to hill, and height to height, "Till"—as Macaulay sings—

> " The proud Peak unfurled the flag o'er Derwent's rocky dales :
> Till, like volcanoes, flamed to heaven, the stormy hills of Wales ;
> Till twelve fair counties saw the blaze on Malvern's lonely height ;
> Till streamed in crimson on the wind the Wrekin's crest of light ;
> Till bright and fierce the star came forth on Ely's lofty fane,
> And town and hamlet rose in arms o'er all the boundless plain ;
> Till Belvoir's lordly towers the sign to Lincoln sent,
> And Lincoln sped the message on, through the broad vale of Trent,
> Till Skiddaw saw the fire that burnt on Gaunt's embattled pile,
> And the red glare on Skiddaw roused the burghers of Carlisle."

But our train has moved on, and we are in a deep and wide cutting, from the sides of which huge blocks of sandstone jut out. The exit from this cutting is singularly abrupt, the train being shot out, as it were, from the side of an almost precipitous rock to the top of a lofty embankment. We here catch our first view of Sutton, its gray church tower crowning the hill, with the fine Town Hall and the pretty turretted school buildings crouching at its feet. Their bright appearance, and sharp outlines, as seen in the clear atmosphere, strike one with surprise from the contrast with the dingy aspect of the big town we have left seven miles behind us. In two or three hundred yards we pull up at the Sutton station, where the line terminates at the foot of a precipitous rock.

One of the attractions of Sutton Park, Blackroot Pool
c. 1863 by Miss Bracken

Postscript

From Rural Sleepiness to Bustling Activity*

By rail the journey to Birmingham only took twenty minutes, and Sutton's popularity as a healthy residential area grew accordingly. The population of the town increased from 4,662 in 1861 to 7,737 in 1881, and in 1869 the *Birmingham Daily Post* proclaimed that the railway was responsible for its passing *'from rural sleepiness to bustling activity'*. It was also responsible for the Park becoming a popular rendezvous for the working people of Birmingham and the Black Country, and the railway company was quick to exploit the Park's all-the-year-round attraction. In 1870, for instance, an advertisement in the *Birmingham Daily Post* for a Christmas trip to the Park ran as follows:

LONDON AND NORTH-WESTERN RAILWAY

Skating on Wyndley Pool, Sutton Coldfield

A CHEAP EXCURSION TRAIN will run from New Street Station at 12 noon and 2.15 p.m. to SUTTON COLDFIELD, THIS DAY (Monday), December 26, and every day during the Frost. Fare there and back including admission to the Royal Promenade and Wyndley Pool, 9d. Covered Carriages.

The Park's popularity prompted Dean Hole to say of Bracebridge Pool, after comparing it favourably with Killarney, that it was:

> " . . . one of the prettiest spots in England, whose tranquil loveliness is a refreshment and a blessing to thousands of our weary artisans."

* Following Sutton's rail link with Birmingham, the population of the town increased from 4,662 in 1861 to 7,737 in 1881, and in 1869 the 'Birmingham Daily Post' proclaimed that the railway was responsible for it passing 'from rural sleepiness to bustling activity'.

Main Sources of Reference

A number of statements made differ from other accounts of the events, so notes referring to sources have been given.

Main sources used were:

A. A. Bracken, *History of the Forest and Chase of Sutton Coldfield,* 1860.

W. K. Riland Bedford, *History of Sutton Coldfield,* 1891, reprinted 1968.

Rex Christiansen, *Regional History of the Railways of Great Britain vol 7—The West Midlands,* David and Charles 1973.

R. K. Dent, *Old and New Birmingham,* 1880, reprinted 1972.

J. Horsfall, *The Ironmasters of Penns,* Roundwood Press 1971.

Stephenson Locomotive Society, *Railways of the West Midlands, a chronology 1808—1954,* 1954.

N. W. Webster, *Britain's First Trunk Line,* Adams and Dart 1972.

Public Record Office: Kew
    Board minutes of the BL&MR and LNWR
    Eckersley and Reed contract
    Board of Trade Inspectors' reports

Warwick County Record Office:
    QS 111 — deposited plans for railway bills.

Sutton Coldfield Library:
    Minute books of the Warden and Society.
    The Railway Bill, a collection of papers including a transcript of the proceedings of the House of Commons Select Committee of 1859. It is in 16 parts, i, ii, 1—9, a—e.

The local collections of Sutton Coldfield and Birmingham Central libraries were extensively used.

---

* Reprinted from *The Royal Town of Sutton Coldfield—A Commemorative History* (Douglas Jones).

Notes to Chapter 1

(RB = Railway Bill)

1. The Vauxhall terminus was near the present Duddeston Station (Webster, p. 70).
2. Dent, p. 449. Dent's account omits the coach 'Triumph', supplied from Webster, p. 95.
3. RB 7, p. 19; deposited plans.
4. RB 6, p. 15.
5. RB b.
6. RB 2, p. 16 and p. 64.
7. Riland Bedford, p. 62.
8. BL&MR Board minutes.
9. Deposited plans.
10. BL&MR Board minutes.
11. LNWR Board minutes.
12. RB 6, p. 6; Riland Bedford.
13. RB 8, p. 2.
14. Riland Bedford, p. 63.
15. Warden and Society minutes.
16. M. Stenton, *Who's Who of British MPs,* 4 vols, 1976.
17. Warden and Society minutes.
18. Dent, p. 505.
19. RB 8, p. 16.
20. Bracken, p. 121.
21. RB 8, p. 20.
22. RB 2a.
23. Horsfall, p. 84.
24. RB 5, p. 7.
25. RB 5, p. 5.
26. Dent, pp. 554—5.
27. RB 8, pp. 5—8.
28. RB 5, p. 7.
29. RB 5, p. 8.
30. RB 5, pp. 9—10.
31. RB 5, p. 23.
32. RB 5, pp. 11—13.
33. RB 5, p. 26.
34. RB 5, p. 46, RB 6, p. 56, iid.
35. RB 5, p. 14.
36. RB 8, p. 22.
37. Warden and Society minutes.
38. RB 5, p. 15, ii.
39. RB 8, p. 29.
40. RB 5, p. 16.
41. RB 8, pp. 10, 23, 24, 26.
42. *Dictionary of National Biography.*
43. RB 8, p. 28.
44. LNWR Board minutes.
45. RB 9, p. 36.

Notes to Chapter 2

(RB = Railway Bill)

1. RB, p. 34.
2. RB 8, pp. 46—7.
3. RB 7, p. 19, deposited plans.
4. RB 6, p. 4, RB 8, p. 20.
5. Deposited plans.
6. RB 5, p. 76.
7. RB 6, p. 80.
8. RB 6, p. 37.
9. RB 6, p. 63, RB 7, p. 23.
10. RB 7, pp. 23—30.
11. RB 6, pp. 43—4.
12. RB 6, p. 11.
13. RB 8, p. 48.
14. RB 6, p. 27.
15. RB 6, p. 10.
16. RB 6, p. 46, RB 9, p. 5.
17. RB 8, p. 42
18. RB 6, p. 40.
19. RB 9, p. 21.
20. RB 7, i.
21. RB 5, p. 16.
22. RB 8, p. 19.
23. RB 6, p. 52.
24. RB 6, pp. 32—6.
25. RB 6, p. 82.
26. Plan in Sutton Library.
27. RB 9, p. 28.
28. RB 9, p. 32.
29. RB 8, p. 49.
30. Memel, now Klaipeda, a Lithuanian seaport on the Baltic.
31. Board of Trade Inspector's report.
32. RB 9, pp. 12—14.
33. RB 6, pp. 49—52.